Love You, Ava Baby

Love You, Ava Baby

The Truth about Life after Losing a Child and How I Found Peace and Joy in the Sorrow

Erin E. Chandler

NEW YORK

LONDON • NASHVILLE • MELBOURNE • VANCOUVER

Love You, Ava Baby

The Truth about Life after Losing a Child and How I Found Peace and Joy in the Sorrow

Published in New York, New York, by Morgan James Publishing in partnership with Difference Press. Morgan James is a trademark of Morgan James, LLC. www.MorganJamesPublishing.com

ISBN 9781642794731 paperback
ISBN 9781642794748 eBook
Library of Congress Control Number: 2019933114

Cover Design by:
Megan Dillon
megan@creativeninjadesigns.com

Interior Design by:
Chris Treccani
www.3dogcreative.net

Morgan James is a proud partner of Habitat for Humanity Peninsula and Greater Williamsburg. Partners in building since 2006.

Get involved today! Visit
MorganJamesPublishing.com/giving-back

Dedication

In honour of my Earth children, Gabriella and Domenic, and
my Spirit child, Ava.
You are the brightest lights in my life and I thank the universe
every day that I am blessed that the three of you are in my life.
You are loved beyond measure, cherished infinitely.

Table of Contents

The Truth about Life after Losing a Child

"Goodbyes are the hardest when the story wasn't over."

– UNKNOWN

Date of Death: July 21, 2010

Never did I ever expect that my life would truly begin with death. Not for one second did I ever think that all of my joy for life would abruptly end on July 21st, as I held my child's lifeless body. And never could I have ever imagined what it really feels like to wake up every morning knowing that my child is dead. I could never have foreseen how many people would devalue my child's life and my own life in the process.

I remember very distinctly eleven years ago when I was told about a co-worker whose daughter had died. I remember thinking, *I wonder what that feels like? I feel so sad for her, how terrible.* Now I know that my attempt at imagining this terrible thing didn't even scratch the surface of what it really feels like. I can truly say that a person cannot imagine nor understand the true devastation of this event... unless they too have experienced the death of their own child. Ever since my daughter passed away, I am brought to tears of great empathy when I hear about the death of any child. To my surprise, I'm crying for *you*. The mothers and fathers who have now been thrust onto a path that no parent wants to take. A path that is fraught with bottomless pits of sorrow and mountains of grief that are followed by more mountains of grief.

I was told over and over that *time heals all wounds.* This is so far from the truth when your child dies. How can time heal a wound that is reopened every day? When my children go to their first day of school, or every birthday, every Christmas, it is a reminder that my daughter isn't there with us. The truth is that time cannot heal the wound of knowing you've been robbed of watching your child grow up. Time cannot heal all of your own hopes and dreams for your child and for your life together, that are no longer possible. Time can't heal your other children's joy at the thought of having a sibling, a partner in crime, that was real but no longer exists for them. Time can't heal all of the special moments that were supposed to happen every passing year. There will be no comforting your child when they fall off their bike for the first time. There will be no first day of kindergarten, or high school, or university. There will be no graduations or weddings to celebrate how far they've come and the person they have grown into. Tell me, how can time heal an entire lifetime of laughter and tears, joy and disappointment, a whole life of a mother's unending love?

We live in a world that puts grieving a child in a tiny box with a neat little bow on top and a little note saying: *Here are the stages of grief, try and be grateful for what you have. P.S.: we estimate X amount of time to get over it and move on because it is really uncomfortable for the rest of us.*

The truth is there is no map to follow after you bury your child, no ten-step program to feel better and accept the totally unacceptable event that has just happened. You'll likely be told about the stages of grief, which will run through the emotions you might feel – and believe me, you will definitely feel all of them, but at one hundred times the intensity that is so gently described. At first I felt comfort in knowing the stages of grief. But after a short time, I realized that I clearly wasn't following the neat and tidy compartmentalized stages of grief that you can expect to go through. This made me feel like I was grieving the wrong way because I wasn't following how they were *supposed* to be. What was wrong with me? And why did no one understand what I was going through? And why on earth didn't anyone tell me that every stage of grief is intricately intertwined within each other and in the most inexplicable ways?

There are moments that I am brought to my knees, knowing that my daughter's life and death are a series of memories forever seared into my heart, my mind, and my soul. Sometimes it is like it was yesterday. Her death was like a WWII bomb being detonated in the middle of my heart, totally annihilating my world as I knew it. I went from a life I thought I loved to being totally blindsided and not understanding anything about anything. All in a matter of 2.5 seconds. Nothing could've prepared me for the devastation of a moment like that, or the destruction that would follow it.

I felt utterly alone. There was no one who could tell me that they understood how it felt to lose a child. I felt total despair and sorrow, crying for days until I was crying on the inside because my body couldn't produce another tear. I felt pure, unadulterated rage at God, Spirit, The Man Upstairs, whomever is in charge, for what had happened to my daughter, my family, and me. There would never be a good enough reason for her death. Why couldn't it have been me instead? What did I do to deserve this, for my family to deserve this? My daughter didn't deserve to die.

And *blame*. For all of the people who crossed my daughter's path in her short life that I felt could've changed their actions, could've taken one more look at the situation, or kept their appointments to see her, or made one different decision that would have resulted in her being alive. I wanted to rewind. With every fibre of my being, I wanted to go back to when she was alive and I could stroke her forehead and rock her to sleep, or soothe her never-ending hiccups. God, I miss those ridiculous hiccups. I'd give anything to hear them from her throat again. I'd give anything to hear her little cry. I'd give anything to hold her, even if for just one last moment. It is the little everyday things that we do that should be cherished. They end up being the most important and filled with the deepest love. Most people miss these moments altogether, taking them for granted. There are some who will spend their entire lives never even knowing the value of these moments.

No one talks about the cloak you wear over your shoulders, made of a thousand bricks that weigh down every bone in your body, every minute of every day. Or how the ache in the middle of your chest is so deep that it hurts to breathe, hurts to get up, hurts to sleep. And the *guilt*. It permeated every corner of my being, every crack in my foundation; guilt for not being able to save her. For not knowing that something was wrong. For not demanding better care when I felt it necessary. It is my fault because I am her mother and I was supposed to be her Protector and now she is gone and I am a complete failure. I don't know that there are any words to accurately describe the suffering of living each day after you've lost a child when there is no space to grieve them and no one to turn to.

The reality of life is the reality of death. Every single human being will experience death, whether it be tomorrow or in seventy-five years. And yet, it's the most misunderstood, least talked about and most uncomfortable thing to talk about for millions of people. Maybe no one wants to talk about it because it is too intense, too real, and too painful to look it in the eye and just be there. Well, I want to talk about this. I need to talk about this. You need to talk about this and to know that you are not alone. There are people who are right there with you. You are part of the club that no one wants to be a part of, but here you and I are. What you don't know yet is that this club is filled with the most resilient, loving, and beautiful people, who walk with their heads held high, honouring their children every day of their lives, and loving fiercely despite loss. And you will, too. Let your heart be soothed by my journey. Find comfort in knowing that I understand how you feel. Build strength knowing that your true feelings and grief are real and need to be honoured.

You are not alone, love, not abandoned. Just lean on me.

Chapter 1

Life, as I Knew it, Has Just Ended

"Ever has it been that love knows not its own depth until the hour of separation."

– **Khalil Gibran**

My daughter Ava was born on June 14th, 2010. Beautiful and perfectly imperfect, with heart defects. She successfully underwent heart surgery on her first day in this world.

We were discharged only ten days after her heart surgery. I felt on top of the world driving home with my little girl, despite the site of surgery on the side of her chest being open, despite the blood clot in one of her legs. I can't describe the elation I felt, knowing that my daughter would live, her heart would heal. In my heart I believed that this hospital and all the doctors there were the be all and end all. After this, I trusted them 110 percent. Life was amazing and miracles did happen. And then my miracle child was taken away five short weeks later.

Her body feels cooler than normal, she was crying all morning and this afternoon she doesn't seem to want to eat. What should I do?

I had waited almost an hour on the phone to ask this question, as the head doctor had just started his rounds at the Children's Hospital when I called. I could taste the fear on the end of my words when I said them. They had cancelled Ava's appointment to monitor her, which had been scheduled the day before – the doctor was on vacation.

The nurse replied with a calm, reassuring tone. "We've spoken with the doctor leading the rounds and we think she sounds okay. Maybe to be on the safe side take her in to your local hospital and they can have a quick look. It sounds like she will be just fine."

I felt a wave of calm settle over me after hearing the nurse's voice and those words. Doing exactly as I was told, I hopped in the car to go the hospital for reassurance that I didn't feel I needed anymore after talking to the nurse.

My partner, Evan, had dropped me off at the hospital with Ava and left for a business meeting. We truly believed that this was just a precautionary visit because the Children's Hospital thought that she sounded like she was fine. When I walked in, there was a nurse at the door asking if she could help me.

"I just got off the phone with the Children's Hospital, who told me to come in here. My daughter is a cardiac patient," I said.

She immediately whisked me to a hospital bed, asking what day she had cardiac surgery. She started calling in other nurses and asking me more questions. And with each question she asked, the more frantic the people around me became. Panic started to seep in the more they rushed around, the more I realized something was wrong and that these people didn't know what they were doing. It was total chaos.

A hospital coordinator rushed in, telling me I needed to call someone, I needed family to be there with me. I was then told I needed to leave because they were going to intubate her and put her on life support, because she was struggling to breathe on her own. They ushered me into a closed room away from the chaos.

I sat in this room for forty-five minutes. Forty-five minutes of begging God to help my daughter. Calling Evan over and over with never an answer. I left messages, *Please come to the hospital, something's wrong,* over and over. Forty-five minutes of isolation in a cold grey room, crying, praying, panicking. My last call in that room was to my dad. Between my sobs, I told him that we were at the hospital with Ava and that I was scared, I didn't know what was going on. I don't even know what my father said, but I do know that I left that room feeling like the Children's Hospital was the expert and I trusted them. This hospital was just a bunch of nurses panicking and Ava would be just fine. I wiped my tears away along with my feeling of dread and walked out that door, over to my daughter.

I would hold on tightly to this feeling as I watched my daughter's chest rising and falling with the machine. She was trying to cry out. My baby was crying out and the tubing was moving around and coming up. "We're going to sedate her so that she is more comfortable and the tubing doesn't dislodge – we had some trouble getting it in," the doctor said. Sedated, Ava became still again. Her little eyes would dry out, staring blankly before I had to ask the doctor to close her eyes, they were so dry and looked so painful. I was still hanging on to that same feeling, sitting, waiting, observing as if I was on the outside, listening to every word for a clue, a direction. I would watch as a group of nurses congregated at the table in the middle of the ER. I overhear them talking to each other about how they don't have the proper blood pressure medication for a child. Asking each other what they calculated the adult blood pressure medication to be for a seven-pound newborn infant. Each one gave a different calculation, then giggled at not knowing how they all got a different dosage. They had already given my baby girl this drug! It didn't make sense to me that I was watching and hearing this conversation in front of me. I couldn't figure out how to feel about this, whether I needed to say something or not. I just watched in disbelief and refocused on the hope of knowing that my daughter would be fine.

And again, I would clench that feeling between my teeth when the doctor called Ava's hospital, only to be told that they would not accept her. *They don't feel it's an issue with her heart, so they won't accept her for a transfer at this time. Once Ava is stable we will send her to a different children's hospital. We can't find the cause of the erratic heartbeat or the low blood pressure. It's all right though. I am a doctor from that same children's hospital, so I'm familiar with them.*

The people who saved her life were now deserting her, deserting me. Despite the feeling of betrayal at their failure to follow my daughter in her time of need, I held steadfast to that same thought, that same feeling, *Ava will be just fine. She was a successful heart surgery patient. If she could survive that, this is nothing. They said she would be just fine. It isn't her heart.*

Hours passed, waiting and watching. Tests that showed nothing. Evan finally arrived and I needed to keep holding this feeling of security and safety, knowing that if I let it go I would break and it would all be a lie, so I looked to him to calm me. I tried to lighten the mood and laugh just so I could pretend that everything really was going to be okay. If I believed it and acted like it, then it would be that way. This got me looks of disgust from some of the nurses at the hospital, but I didn't bat an eye because I was desperately clinging to the belief that Ava would be just fine and nothing was going to change that.

In the wee hours of the next morning, nothing had changed with Ava's status. The nurses from another children's hospital arrived in an ambulance and asked us to go make our way to their hospital ahead of them. "No, I want to go with her in the ambulance," I stated, but I was met with the nurse's abrupt answer.

"No, you can't. Meet us there. Bring everything you'll need for her stay at the hospital, at least a week's worth of things for her. When she is stable we'll transfer her by ambulance."

I felt like I'd been slapped in the face by this miserable woman, but I put on my brave face and said nothing to her. I did as I was told and we went home to pack Ava's bags for her stay at the new children's hospital. The nurse's acknowledgement that we would be staying at another hospital also said to me, that my daughter Ava would be just fine.

Once home, I realized I hadn't showered in a week. I had been so preoccupied with cleaning and packing Ava's wounds, administering her needles every day, measuring the food she took in, seeing the nurses and appointments, and all that is required for post cardiac surgery for a tiny little baby, that I didn't take the time to take care of myself. Who am I kidding, I barely slept, let alone bathed, when I had a five-week-old baby, never mind a major organ surgery to monitor and tend to. I needed to shower after packing. I needed to wash away the feeling of despair, the knowing that this was an unexpected twist, if only to wash away the smell of the hospital that had permeated my clothes and the tears that had soaked my cheeks and sleeves of my shirt. In the shower I was overcome with a sudden feeling of such sorrow, and I started to cry. I could not move, I couldn't get out, all I could do was sob and I couldn't stop. It wasn't until Evan came into the bathroom, pulling back the shower curtain saying I'd been in there a really long time and we had to go, that I became aware of where my body was again and what I needed to do. Stepping out of the shelter of the shower, it was time to face the fear and go back into the danger zone of life. I put my clothes on and left for the hospital.

Fifteen minutes into the drive, with Evan speeding down the highway, the phone rang. It was the nurse from the children's hospital.

"Where are you? You were supposed to be here before the ambulance. Things are not looking good. Please get here as fast as you can. But drive carefully." There was sadness in her voice mixed with irritation. My partner and I looked at each other with dread, fear, and an innate knowing that our lives might never be the same. He slowed down the car and we grabbed each other's hands and drove the next thirty minutes in total silence, doing exactly the speed limit on the highway. This felt like the longest thirty minutes of my life. Going so slow, as fast as we could.

A nurse met us at the door and curtly said, "Follow me." We walked into the hospital room to see a team of young people doing CPR on my baby girl. It was like walking into a movie, surreal. They were pushing so hard on her chest that her little body seemed to be jumping off the gurney every time they did a compression. "We've been doing CPR for twenty minutes with no sign of resuscitation," the doctor told us in a low voice.

"STOP!" I cried out, "Let me hold her."

They backed away from her slowly as I picked her tiny little body up and wrapped her in the hospital sheet and put her chest onto my chest, skin to skin.

I just need to put her on me, close to me, and she will warm up and she will be okay. Everything is going to be okay. She just needs to feel my heartbeat with hers and she will know that she's okay. She can do this. I can do this, I thought.

"Take the tubes out of her mouth," Evan said through his tears. We laid her down and gently guided the tube out from her mouth. I picked her up and she slowly exhaled, her chest falling. My heart leapt into my mouth, *She's breathing! They're wrong! She's breathing! Come on baby, you can do this, one more time! One more time, Ava. I'll get closer – listen to me breathe. You can do this.*

No! Please. Please, God, Please. Don't take my baby. I can do this. Please!

I truly believed that I could will my daughter to breathe again. I believed with all my heart that this was not the end. Not how her life would end. Not how my role as a mother to her would end. I would later discover that my moment of loss and sorrow in the shower was actually the time when my daughter first lost all vital signs in the ambulance. I would also learn that the team doing CPR on her had broken her ribs from the weight of pushing so hard.

The sorrow and despair that blankets a human being after the death of a child drowns out all signs of life, the mundane everyday things to the joyful sound of a child's laughter, they are muted, they exist only in the background, unheard, unfelt in this type of grief. It is like you are in a vacuum canister, deafened by the incessant drone of sorrow and crippled by the intense emotions that are swirling and slamming against you in the canister that is you. It feels unending, out of control, and erratic. Rolling waves of emotion so intense, you can't get up. So forceful that they choke you, pulling you under with no indicator of when you'll be able to take a breath again. This intensity of being unable to function went on for three months before I could see that I needed help, that I couldn't go on like that.

During the first few weeks the police would request a toxicology report and confiscate things from our home as 'evidence.' But they never looked into the hospitals or the nurses whose care Ava had been in, nor into the cancelled appointments and failure of the children's hospital to monitor her progress. I was also desperate for answers to why my daughter died. Was it her heart? If they hadn't cancelled her appointment would she still be alive? Why are the police investigating me and not investigating the hospital? And why are so many people in the medical community changing their stories after her death? There were so many things that didn't add up. Her cause of death was ruled as natural, acute pulmonary hypotension. I fought this with fierceness in my heart. I searched for people with expertise that could help me fight for the truth. I needed to know the truth. I needed to know the why. And I needed someone to give me a reason. This need would be the only thing keeping me going ... for a while.

And then I knew I needed to find help. I wasn't functioning. When I was able to seek out help, it would end up being from the wrong people, people who really couldn't support me or simply did not understand, nor want to understand. Evan and I were met with so many obstacles, so many unanswered questions. It felt like not one person could hold a space for me to feel all that you feel after your child dies. I was repeatedly met with emotional walls from others with comments and people who made it clear that I shouldn't be feeling so sad and angry about this loss and that I should move on, or feel lucky, or simply not talk about it. Here is where the bereaved are often abandoned. Here is where our culture fails to support each other in our greatest time of need, our deepest wells of sorrow. Here is where we start to drown in sorrow and experience more damaging events that can keep us down in the despair that replays in the minds and hearts of a bereaved parent.

The lack of understanding and support would sink me so deep in grief that it manifested into my body, my relationships, and my family. In my vulnerability of shock and grief, I accepted that there was no place for grief and that I simply couldn't talk to anyone about it, as this was my experience. So I stuffed it down, shut my mouth, and pasted a smile on my face. For a while I was able to fool myself, but then the secondary losses would start to slowly pile up one after the other, year after year. I got sicker and sicker, experiencing a mysterious illness that no expert could explain. I lost my house that I had spent years working for, I lost my health, and I lost all the relationships that mattered to me. My final breaking point was discovering that my partner, Evan, had betrayed me both emotionally and physically while I was sick. He was the only person in this world that I felt understood all that we had been through, the only person I thought really saw me. This was when I totally stopped functioning. I no longer felt safe or loved in this world or by God. Without support that felt safe and being unable to reach out for help, I sank. Mentally and physically unable to help myself, I hit rock bottom. I gave up, I no longer had any fight left in me, no desire to know why or to grow.

The giving up was my surrendering to the truth of my life, of my daughter's death, of all that was. I didn't want any of the facts of my life to be true, it was just too painful, too real, too much loss. This surrender was the opening for Spirit to show me a true miracle – That my daughter was with me all the time, joyfully alive in her soul and trying desperately to help me, to guide me, to heal me and to lead me to more joy and love than I ever thought possible. A divinely orchestrated messenger of truth that shocked me, humbled me, and held me in love and safety. This gave me renewed strength to keep going, to fight for myself, to fight to live. It showed me that our beliefs cripple our ability to live, to love, to grieve – it proved to me that death is not the end. That the body is merely a moment in time, a vessel. But our souls, who we really are, are unending and everywhere. My daughter Ava is alive and living, just not in her body. Yes, you read that right.

Ava would begin to show me the miracles of life and death. To make herself known and the truth be felt. This is what I want to share with you, to show you, to help you, to heal your broken heart. This sorrow and your heartbreak do not define you. There is deep joy in this understanding and purpose in its truth. And it opens the door to a complete realignment in who you thought you were. It allows you to unveil the truth and learn the simple lessons that let you truly live and love in peace and joy. I'm living proof that you can heal your heart and realign your whole life, love, perspective and rebuild in peace. Know that you are being held in infinite love and can follow the same path of healing that my daughter led me to.

Chapter 2

Surrendering to What Is

"Transformation happens on the other side of Surrender."
– Unknown

I truly believed with all my heart and soul that everything would be okay because I, or God or Spirit, all had the power to make that happen in those last moments of Ava's life. I thought that I could control the living and the dying in the present moment with sheer will. I could not see past that moment. The shock and disbelief would block out conversations, where I was, how I got there. I couldn't find these things in my memory. Just breathing in the first three months is the only thing I could really do. Interactions with people in this time frame either heightened my fear and despair or were totally gone from my thoughts, as if they never even happened.

At my daughter's funeral, I don't remember how I got there. I was just suddenly there, in slow motion, just like a Charlie Chaplin movie. We decided to write a letter of gratitude to our closest friends and family and read it to them at the church. In reading this, I was shaking uncontrollably, suddenly recognizing that I wasn't reading it, I was actually having a full conversation with my best friend in my head that went like this, *Jeannie, something is wrong, this isn't real, we're not supposed to be here. Why are we here, I want to leave, please let's go now.* When in real life, I was reading the letter to this group of people - two realities at once, like watching both at the same time, like it wasn't me but two movies playing over top of each other.

Months and even years after the funeral, the people who had attended would tell me the one thing they would always remember and they all said the same thing. As my daughter's casket closed, I screamed out. A pure, anguish-filled, guttural scream that cut straight to their souls. They said they could still hear it and feel the emotion in it today, just the knowing that someone they knew felt like that, that no one should ever feel the way that this scream felt deep in their souls.

A scream that I didn't even know came out of me.

Three months after my daughter died, I attempted to find some help, for anyone who lived near me who had lost a child. I scoured the internet for anyone who could tell me the depth of what I was feeling, that they had felt it too. I found nothing that was an authentic and raw feeling that was close to mine. There were lots of websites and lots of information on how you might feel and to be gentle with yourself when you're grieving. These were like an insult to the intensity of how I felt. The unfairness, the guilt, the blame, the rage ... and a 180-degree swing between rage and sheer sadness that left me lying on the floor crying out for hours.

I felt so alone. How could there be so few people going through this? So few resources for this? Why could I not find genuine help? I felt I had been deserted by God, abandoned by my tribe, with nowhere to turn. I struggled to keep it together and reached out to the only grieving group I could find. All my faith was hanging on this one single group to help me. Instead of these people supporting me in my grief, they told me that I should feel lucky that my daughter had lived for five and a half weeks. I'm sorry, but honestly, who in their right mind would actually feel *lucky* that their child lived, when they had just died? I was so vulnerable after my daughter's death that I believed them. I believed them that I didn't have the right to feel so sad, so unlucky, so cheated, and feel such despair.

Life and people just kept piling on more reasons that I shouldn't be sad. Like the police detective, who when I arrived at the station and asked about the progress of the investigation into Ava's cause of death, smirked at me. "Why? Are you making a scrapbook of her?" he asked. In what world is it funny that my child is dead? And what does a picture scrapbook have to do with a police officer doing his job of investigating my daughter's death? In one snide sentence, he had told me that my daughter's life had no value and that I had no value, and how amusing he found that to be. His statement would completely shut down any ability I might have had to deal with my daughter's death.

His delivery of that sentence would define me and then slowly help destroy me over the next seven years.

Society, cultural beliefs, religions, and all sorts of people don't allow us to feel all these feelings. This became abundantly clear to me. So I stuffed them down so deep that I did not speak about my daughter for long periods over the years, pretending that everything was okay and it didn't really matter. And the rage and grief I wasn't allowed to feel sunk to the depths of my soul and slowly deteriorated my physical and mental health. And every specialist I saw, over a four-year period, could not explain why I was getting sicker and sicker, but did feel that a pill might solve it, that I could use an antidepressant because my child died. No antidepressant could ever fill the hole in my heart, nor mask the depth of my sorrow.

Grief can have two faces. Every day for seven years, I pasted a smile on my face for each day that was so bleak and full of this suffering that it permeated my soul under that smile. I would crumble the moment I stepped back into my home. My family seeing the true face of grief, the most broken part of me day in and day out, while I accommodated the rest of the world by pretending it was okay, so that they wouldn't be uncomfortable. This facade could only stay for so long before it destroyed me. Grief will be heard no matter what. When I finally gave up, unable to move or think or feel anything but pain, I screamed at the top of my lungs, *I give up. I surrender.* I would finally surrender to what was. This is the only way to move forward. The only way to grieve. The only way to live again and the only way to stitch the pieces of your broken heart together. No, your heart will not be the same, and no your life will not be the same.

The moment your child took their last breath was the moment the person you thought you were died. Surrender to this. That person does not exist anymore, no matter how much you deny it, fight it, and try to put it back together. In order to rebuild you must destroy every building, every foundation that the old you was built upon. Only when this is all in ashes, burnt to the ground, a life that was simply a thought, will you be able to start building from a foundation of truth and love. Surrender is the key to peace and joy, the door that is waiting for you to walk through it.

Surrendering and letting all of the walls fall to the ground is what is required for a miracle to grow from the rubble. When I finally surrendered, I understood that I would never be the same. That I had the opportunity to see the truth in death. That I didn't have to suffer like this anymore. Without surrendering to what is, you are fighting the truth. Regardless of how much you cannot accept it, at some point you have to surrender in order to move through it. Again, surrender is the key to moving forward. It is the first gift to start the healing process. Without it, you cannot heal.

This surrender was the gateway for me to see the truth. A brave, loving soul took a huge risk in approaching me to tell me that my daughter Ava and my grandmother were coming to her every day, crying to her and begging her to help me, to tell me they were there with me. My grandmother, June, and my daughter, Ava, are both dead in every way, according to our culture and taught beliefs. But in truth, they are alive and living, transformed from body back to soul, which is all we really are. This woman recounted with shocking accuracy my innermost thoughts and feelings, letting me know that Ava feels everything that I feel, hears everything that I think. This would open the flood gates of my heart, and everything that had sat and stewed in the dark for seven years from the depths of my soul - I finally gave myself *permission* to feel all the sorrow, the anger, the pain and the disappointment.

For me, this was the beginning of grieving my daughter's death. I would spend months of moving through all of the obstacles that had been placed before me, one by one, unpacking each tattered piece. And each thing that I unpacked beckoned me to really look at it. To feel it, to give it a place in my heart where it could be held and loved. To move with it and let it guide me to the reasons, the purpose, how it shaped me, and what I was going to do with it. To let go of the control that made the suffering so intense. To grieve. To forgive. To love.

I was able to take back my power. I was given an avenue to connect through Spirit with my daughter, who opened doors and showed me what life and love truly are. I found a way to walk through the anguish and the sorrow by facing it and feeling it without my judgement and the judgement of others. I discovered that talking and sharing with someone who has walked this path of child loss can bring you more comfort, validation, and purpose than I'd ever imagined. I learned how to step up and face the pain and let people help me, with someone who supported my grief, accepting where I was with no judgement and holding my heart with gentle hands every step of the way. I want to show you through my journey how you too can find peace in surrender and feel joy in the sorrow. Great purpose can be grown from the seeds of pain that were planted in your heart when your child died. If you follow the signs of Spirit, the obstacles that are laid before you will disappear, and the mountains that feel unclimbable will suddenly become climbable. Take comfort in reading the realness of heartache and despair, knowing that you are not alone. Take my hand and feel the hope that comes from each mountain, each loss, each hurt and every tear. Know that these mountains indeed can be conquered one step at a time, with help and love and compassion. Your answers lie within. Your heart aches to mend itself. Your soul is showing you the way. Do not resist the wind that ripped the roof off of your house, the fear that tries to hold you down in the darkness of the basement. Follow the path of love and Spirit that wants to guide all mothers and fathers – this is where you'll start to heal. Release the resistance, surrender to what is.

When there isn't a safe space for grief and all the emotions that come with it, it can destroy you, force you to resist everything that is needed to heal. I want to hug you – I truly feel your pain and suffering. There is no magic pill that will make you feel better. But I'm going to show you that if we walk through this together, that you will get to the other side of grief. Where there is deeper love, true peace and acceptance and the ability to move forward in your life, with joy and with your child rooting for you every step of the way. There is a light shining for you from the lighthouse across the sea. If you'll just look for the glimmer of it, picture it in your mind, I promise you it's there. Deep within your broken heart is where you'll find it, just like I did.

Chapter 3

Abandoned

The truth about life after losing a child is that it is so emotionally intense that others around you who have never experienced such a loss just don't know how to support you. And their discomfort is so overwhelming that they don't know what to say, so they say nothing. And then there are those that think they're helping while trying to resolve their own discomfort of your grief, which results in them saying and doing the most obscure and painful things. I too have been on the other side of grief as the onlooker so mired in discomfort that I did nothing, stumbling on my words, looking for an escape from the heaviness of the other person's sorrow. But that was before my daughter passed away. Before I could see why we are all taught to run from death. As you'll see in this chapter, the misunderstanding and abandonment of the bereaved can reveal itself within moments of death and in many different ways.

The Cold and Technical Side of Death

When the coroner came into the hospital room and was going through Ava's medical history with me while I held her lifeless body, I was in shock. Everything was moving in slow motion, like I was watching myself from afar, not really hearing anything, but overhearing my own voice – like I was an observer rather than a participant in what was happening.

I cried in the room as he moved through questions about my daughter, about me, about my history. In my early twenties I had ended two pregnancies. The irony of my ignorance back then about how valuable life actually is, was not lost on me. *God is punishing me for not valuing life as I should have*, I thought. This was like a punch to the diaphragm, knocking the wind out of me. I wept with my head down, seeing my mistakes. I wept for all three of my babies now. I wept for all the things that never came to pass through my own choices and now through God's choices. All the regret, all of the shame. Eighteen years ago, I felt that I had no other option but to not have these children. And now I see that it was simply a choice that I cannot take back. The coroner quickly caught my change in tears, saying, "I'm sorry if I upset you." I wanted to lash out at him. Upset me? I'm holding my dead child in my arms and he thinks he has upset me? The feeling of persecution and guilt, grief, shock and loss is what upsets me. I held myself hostage for my past decisions for the next seven years. Punishing myself for this. It would take those seven years to see that everything happens for a reason, that there are no mistakes, and I was not being punished by God in any way, shape or form. I couldn't have learned the gift that life truly is any other way.

Evan and I left the hospital after hours of holding Ava, left her there in that cold sterile room. We drove home in silence, so thick and heavy. There simply were no words, no comforting each other in the truth. Within minutes of arriving home, two homicide detectives came into the house and politely advised us that we should collect a few personal items and direct them to my daughter's things, which would be collected as evidence. It never occurred to me at the time, being in shock, that I was suspected as having something to do with my daughter's death, for a potential homicide investigation. They followed us room to room, watching while we packed a few things and left for the police station to be interviewed. Again, I believed they were just trying to help us and they would figure out where everything went wrong. I had no idea there would be so many lies and so much misinformation that would shroud my daughter's life and death in a mystery. A mystery that I would never be able to solve. A mystery that lit the fire underneath my desire to know why, to know the truth. Not knowing how your child had died or who is responsible is so difficult. So painful. Only surrendering to this not knowing would show me that there was an easier way. That greater strides are made when time is allowed to work its way through the universe's plan. Moving through the question of why, I have written an entire chapter dedicated to this enormous question, that will help you through it.

Because we were being investigated, an autopsy was done immediately. When the autopsy concluded that her death was from natural causes, acute pulmonary hypotension, I shuddered deep in my heart with a knowing that this was not the truth, not the cause. When we were cleared to go home, we would pull up to a house that was taped off with police investigation tape still there. A house that was no longer a home. I no longer wanted to be in this place. The mail lady would come the next morning and ask what was going on. The police officer stationed at my home for the last week had been a high school friend of hers and had told her that my home was a crime scene investigation. This was the first part of the decimation of my belief in our bodies of protection. These were men and women who I held in high esteem, who were supposed to protect us all - but they weren't protecting me or my daughter. I told the mail lady that my daughter had passed away and that she had been a cardiac patient. The mail lady gasped at this, divulging that her daughter too was a cardiac patient at that same hospital but was alive and well.

My rage at being defamed, devalued, and judged as a murderer for no apparent reason would saturate every fibre of my being, knowing the unjust, inappropriate, uncalled for actions and words that the police used were the truth of who they really were, what they represented. This was when I realized that my belief that the police will keep me and my children safe was a lie. The institution I believed in wholeheartedly was a farce. I felt I could trust no one. The invisible safety net that I had always thought would catch me had been cut open.

The Elephant in the Room

Ava's funeral was, in a sense, my funeral too. Family and friends would stay away and the odd time I would see them, no one dared speak of my daughter. She was the elephant in the room. Ava was always the topic that sat heavily in the air of the room with no one willing to say the truth or acknowledge that she was even here, or had lived or breathed. This destroyed me in so many ways. It made me feel that they too did not value her life enough to talk about her. The things that were actually said to me were excruciatingly painful and quite heartless.

You need to get over this. Be grateful for the daughter that you do have. You're lucky she lived as long as she did. You knew she was going to die because she was sick, so it's not that bad. At least she was only a baby. I'm sorry for your loss. I feel worse than you because my husband died.

Yes. These are things that people said to me. People I loved dearly, people who were acquaintances, neighbours, you name it. Everyone had something to say that devalued how I felt and the magnitude of what had just been lost. The finiteness of death. An entire lifetime cremated into a tiny jar of soft grey ashes. Not one person could hold a space for me to sit in this sorrow, this reality, this truth. I felt like no one cared enough to sit in this with me. But the truth is that they did care, they just didn't know *how* to sit in this with me. They had no idea how to fix it or how to help me, so they tried to tell me to look at the positive so that I wouldn't feel bad or negative. If all these people, both trained professionals, friends, and family members, told me that I shouldn't be feeling the way I was feeling, then they must be right. There must be something wrong with me, that I felt this way, that I couldn't get out of bed. That I couldn't look at other people's babies and young children without being angry at them, that I couldn't go a day without crying for hours on end. And so it continued, a mixed bag of either totally not acknowledging what had happened in my life or saying horrible one-liners that cut me to the core. Here is the truth in this experience: you cannot see the positive without acknowledging the negative. Joy cannot come from pain that is not felt, not honoured. Truth can only be discovered when we are willing to face the lie.

When Help Really Isn't Help

I had decided to join group therapy for parents who had lost an infant, the only support I could find. The women in my group were deep in the throes of grieving, with such rawness and vulnerability, so heavily weighted with sorrow and despair. All of them had infant loss through their pregnancy, most within a month of their due dates, and one mother's son died within days of being born. We gathered together, all of us broken, trying to make sense of the sorrow, the why. All lost in their own grief. I was the only person in my group who had a child that settled into a routine, and had overcome great adversity with heart surgery, and unexplainably died weeks later. This type of closed group peer facilitating is intended to hold a space for all the feelings of grief with people who have had a similar loss. Driving to that first meeting, my fear and my sorrow were thick, the air sucked out of the room as we all sat down for the first meeting. Each of us broken and hoping that this place and these people could relieve some of the pain, understand it, share it.

Initially I welcomed the once-a-week meetings, but when they decided to get together outside of the group, they all decided and agreed that I was luckier than them. They told me I was lucky because I got to spend time with my daughter and live with her, get to know her. My heart sank at this and my feeling of utter aloneness returned with a deeper hurt. I felt unsafe again to voice my pain, my hurt, my regrets without someone telling me in some way that I shouldn't feel that way. Even with these other grieving mothers I was not understood, my feelings and loss devalued by the people that I wanted so badly to feel the weight of the grief with, to walk that footpath with me. But that would never come to pass as I simply stopped corresponding and left them behind me – I could not look them in the eye, my hurt was so great. I never told them how deeply that hurt me, and I'm sure they would never have recognized that their thoughts had devalued my grief and my loss. They were simply voicing something that they wished they could've experienced with their child, that they could compare to. I think about these women often, wishing and hoping that they have picked up the broken pieces of their lives after the deaths of their own children and have found the peace that I have found.

A New Life Requires a New Perspective

My "new" life in the aftermath of my daughter's death was unbearable on the best of days, weighted with shame, guilt, rage, and sheer sorrow that felt unending. This is what every day felt like for seven years. I've learned that we use words and phrases without thought behind what emotion is driving it, or how it affects another person. Words hurt. Bottom line. They can cut you to the soul and shape your core beliefs, values, processes, and perspectives. One statement can define a person on every level. We don't think before we speak, nor observe before reacting. We are walking, talking by-products of our childhood, our parents, our siblings, our teachers, our friends and our own unique personal experiences that each of us go through.

Every judgement, every word we hear lines the inner soul with a layer of belief. We are taught our belief systems, to fit into the mold that is ironically deemed normal. Nothing is normal when your child dies. Lots of people will have a judgement or an opinion on how you should feel or how to fix this. There is no fixing the finiteness of death. What if they really thought about what they wanted to say to someone who has just lost a child? I can tell you, I don't want to hear "I'm sorry for your loss" over and over. This term seems so trite in the face of the unbearable sorrow and despair you feel. It downplays and discredits the grieving. And yet when another bereaved parent says this to me – they are truly sorry, for they know the sorrow and what that loss means because they are living it. I have been on both sides of this fence, and can now see that the statement "I'm sorry for your loss" had one purpose every time I said it: to make myself feel more comfortable in the face of such intense emotion and loss and grief.

Being the recipient of this statement over and over has changed my feeling of it, my awareness of the reason I say this statement and what it feels like to hear it. That statement never reaches my heart, it doesn't resonate with me. I don't want people to be sorry that my daughter is dead and brush that feeling from their lives because they are uncomfortable. They are uncomfortable because my daughter is dead. And yes, that word is abrasive to hear. It pushes up against the very foundation of what we fear. I used to cringe at the word "dead" and the discomfort of it. Isn't that why we don't use that word in grief counselling, or when we talk about our loved one? Because it's so final. Instead we use the terms "passed away" or "loss" as gentle ways of saying the same thing – "dead." Or could it be that we as human beings inherently know deep in the very being of our infinite souls, that death really isn't the finite, end of all life thing that we as a society have deemed it to be. Why is this word so abhorred? Shouldn't it be revered with awe, love, and Spirit? Like the tree's leaves dying off in the fall, only to regenerate in the spring. They have mastered the art of letting go, the cycle of life, the peeling off of leaves that have grown, lived, and died – an innate knowing that every leaf served a purpose for the greater good of the tree and the universe – only to find that each leaf would come full circle, to give nutrients to the earth that fed the roots of this very tree. And then, in the melting of the snow of spring, that leaf once again was being reborn, regenerated, rejuvenated into a bigger, stronger, and more vibrant leaf. Nothing is ever truly dead. It is only the physicality, a portion or an aspect of every living thing that dies off. I too have shed my skins of hurt, pain, suffering, and beliefs. My daughter shed her physical body because it died. She didn't die. Her spirit is infinite and in everything, everywhere. She beckons to me through other people that I connect with, through animals, flowers, even random license plates that guide me, direct me, and validate my thoughts, and that she is there with me. Like a collective consciousness, she hears every thought I have, feels every feeling. This knowing alone is a great healer of a shattered Mother's heart. This knowing brings comfort to the comfortless, hope to the endless despair. It gives bereaved mothers and fathers permission to love again, to have joy, to know that they are supported and loved now and forever, infinitely.

If I knew eight years ago, what I know today about life after death and that I get to choose how great or little I will suffer in the face of my pain, I would choose to live in the fullness of love and weep in river of sorrow with gratitude for the gift. It is I who decides what will give me purpose, what will spur me on to love again, to live again. That I have been given the gift of life through death, joy from pain. Deep in my heart with all the proof I need to back it, the unexplainable, the miracles... my path of grieving would have been so drastically different had I had someone to tell me that I could choose, someone to show me how I could move through this and teach me how to get through to the joy and peace. It's true – you can choose your own path. You can choose to walk blindly in suffering, or you can choose to take a hand, a leg up if you will, to light the dark when you dive into the blackness of your heart, so that you can light the fire to resurface more whole than before.

My father told me something that held all the wisdom of death in one sentence which resonated deep within me just three days after my daughter passed away. I remember this moment like yesterday, I feel the rawness of the sorrow in that moment tearing apart my soul. I sat under the maple tree in my parents' backyard and sobbed for hours until my father came beside me and said, "Erin, remember, you aren't crying for her, you are crying for you." Even though I felt the pull of the truth of life in this statement, I couldn't accept it. I couldn't break it down. It was so simple and profound.

I never forgot it, despite not acknowledging it. His words would ruminate for eight years before I could see the truth in the statement. The wholeness of it, the door it opens to our perception of death and how we deal with it, how we treat others' grief. Why human beings are constantly in a state of comparing grief, comparing incomes, comparing stuff, comparing education. We are constantly in a state of comparing who is better, who is sadder, who is bigger and smaller – all because we do not see that we are unique and not meant to be compared, but rather rejoiced in all that one is, and how each of us have something unique to contribute to the world. Comparison drowns out the truth, smothers the soul, and denies each and every one of us the right to be ourselves in truth. Death is a shedding of skin that those of us still here in our physical bodies feel the pain of. It is our pain, our suffering, and also our choice of what we do with it.

When your child dies, your entire world collapses on every level, magnifying every fear that you have as a parent. It is an exquisitely personal process. The sorrow of losing your child, whether they're one-day-old or sixty-years-old, no matter the circumstance, is a journey for the strong, a transformation that you are wholly unprepared for, nor thought you wanted. And yet, the most unwanted thing in a parent's life is the most enlightening, cherished, and rounded experience to walk through, to clean your slate of everything you thought, and rebuild from the deepest sorrow to the greatest joy and only from the unshakable foundation of love. The reflection of who you are, what you believe, and why you believe it, is a realignment of all foundations in your life. Imagine that we were taught that death was not the end, that heaven and hell didn't even exist as a belief system at all. That God and the universe are all-forgiving, all-seeing, all-feeling, that no one gets left behind. Imagine that mistakes and choices you make, regardless of the outcome, are supported and loved, that God and Spirit are connecting with you always. I mean always. That's like a dream come true, when you live every day thinking and feeling the suffering of our taught beliefs on death and dying and all you've lost. Wouldn't that eliminate half our suffering, half our judgements, half our sorrow? Why isn't this the truth we are taught?

You will encounter so many situations and people who will say things to you that discredit your child and their life. Things that devalue all of your feelings, maybe even discredit who you are as a person. And when you do experience it, remember that you are loved. Know with every fibre of your being that you are loved wholly, with no judgement. Feel the sting of their words, and the hurt in your heart. Ask yourself, why does this hurt me so badly? What part of my heart does this hurt? What are their words actually saying to me? Read between the lines and ponder them. Linger in the discomfort, the hurt and shame that you will want to run from. Observe it. Try and put yourself outside of it. Acknowledge those feelings and where they truly stem from in your belief of who you are and your experience in this life. The ability to face these questions and then surrender to your answers with brutal honesty and authenticity allows the weight of it to lift off your shoulders. You will be able to consciously direct yourself to love that part of you so deeply that no one else's words or lies can shake the foundation of this truth you've discovered. This process of acknowledging the pain, deciphering what about it actually hurts, and naming it, observing it. This may take an hour, or days, or months, or even years, like it did for me. Remember, you are truly loved, never forgotten, never alone. Your loved one will walk with you through all of these moments. They want you to discover, to live your life fully, to love yourself as they do, to connect you with others that illuminate your path to healing.

Give yourself the freedom to forgive those who are hurting you with their words and judgments, the painfulness of it – let it all go. I forgive every last one of these people that shamed me, hurt me, compared me, betrayed me, devalued me, and lied to me; I too, have been taught by society to discredit the uncomfortableness of grieving. I forgive myself. I forgive them – for truly, they know not what they do. You need to forgive all those that are painful roadblocks in your path. They are there to show you something, to help you uncover one of your own truths, to move you forward in the grieving process or to show you where you need to examine a belief. If you cannot forgive them, remember you are actually choosing not to. You are choosing to remain in the grips of suffering, of despair. All you have to do is be open to forgiving them. Recognize that your own freedom lies in forgiveness.

Chapter 4

Why?

"Sometimes giving up from trying to understand and becoming comfortable with not knowing is the gift of freedom."
– Eckhart Tolle

A lot of my journey has been heavily weighted with the question of "Why?"

I know the who, the what, the where ... but the why eludes me, always seeming just out of reach. Why did it happen, why is this a part of my story? Why do I deserve a lifetime sentence of sorrow and despair? Why does no one care like I do about my daughter's death? Why can't I fix this? Why couldn't I save her? Why did they lie about her condition? Why won't anyone help me? This simple three letter word, "Why," is so complex and often the most unanswered question for so many people who are grieving a child. It is the question of all philosophers, all scientific investigation. We are a species that is searching for the why in every belief that we have about life, death, our family, our spirituality, religion, and everything else under the sun.

Be forewarned of this unnerving and seemingly important, need to know, question of Why. It can consume you. If you get stuck on the why, and many of us do, just know that it can eat you alive if you let it. I am living proof of this. Let me show you how letting go of this and surrendering to God, the universe, and Spirit is a deeply peaceful gift.

The events that led up to my daughter's death were the most charged with regret and questioning of why this happened – like I could go back and put the puzzle pieces together so that it made sense. We can't always make sense of the senseless.

During Ava's recovery after her surgery, I went once a week with her to a highly experienced and trusted paediatrician in our community, who monitored her progress after being discharged from the children's hospital. Five days prior to her death, we saw this paediatrician. He said he was concerned that she wasn't gaining any weight and her blood pressure was difficult to obtain. He asked me when her next appointment was because he felt she needed to be seen back at the cardiac unit sooner rather than later. Fortunately, Ava's appointment with the cardiologist and the other specialists was already scheduled in four days. Both of us concluded that four days would be good timing for her to be seen, but that we shouldn't wait longer than that. I felt reassured.

When I returned home though, I received a message from the children's hospital telling me that they were cancelling her scheduled appointment because the doctor was going on vacation. I called them back immediately. The receptionist let me know that she had rescheduled Ava's follow up appointment for another month away. I told her in detail about the paediatrician's request that they see her. It didn't matter to me if it was with a different cardiologist. All that mattered was that she needed to be seen and there was concern. I spent twenty minutes arguing with this woman. My agitation grew with every pushback she gave me. She would not budge, would not offer me any way to get my daughter seen, despite my pleading. So the receptionist made the medical decision that my daughter could wait for another month to be seen. She made the decision not to ask anyone with medical training if that was an appropriate call given the circumstance of the paediatrician's request. She made those decisions in that phone call, like I knew nothing. My daughter took her last breath a day and a half after that scheduled appointment, that was cancelled for a vacation. I would later discover while poring through my daughter's medical records that the cardiology unit specifically noted that my daughter was to be monitored as an outpatient very closely, due to her age, additional medical issues, blood clot, and the fact that she was being discharged at just ten days old, following cardiac surgery. This was a red flag – I was frozen the moment I read it. An all-knowing that this was not right hit me like a ton of bricks. Why was the receptionist allowed to make that decision, technically a medical decision? Why did one person's vacation take precedence over my daughter being seen at all, by anyone? Why?

At the request of the police, the paediatrician who monitored Ava's progress released his dictation of this follow up appointment from five days before her death. His account on paper of what he observed and what his recommendations were from that day was the total opposite of what had actually happened at her appointment. He claimed that she was steadily gaining weight in proportion to the expectation of her growth. That she seemed very healthy and had good pallor and heart sounds. He stated that he had no concerns for her medical condition at that time. This was another red flag, like a giant stone lodged in the pit of my stomach. I knew that something wasn't right. He was an excellent doctor and did everything that he could possibly do. At no point did I ever feel he was negligent or did not take action when it was called for. Why would he lie? Why?

My first red flag that had started the why questions was remembering that at the hospital, the nurses had discussed not having the appropriate blood pressure medication for a child this age, and had altered the adult medication to a level that was supposed to be safe for her. I distinctly remembered them saying that they each worked out a different dosage that would be acceptable for an infant – and this was after they had already given her the blood pressure medication. And my daughter's autopsy report listed the cause of death as acute pulmonary hypotension. Blood pressure. When we realized this, Evan and I went back to the police station indicating that we wanted to give them additional information and concerns we had from the hospital. We told them an exact recount of the nurses' words after the fact. It wouldn't matter anyways. The police only investigated us. The coroner did not feel any other investigation was warranted. And the regional coroner, who had the authority to request a full inquest into her death, would also refuse any further investigation unless additional pertinent information was brought to light. The children's hospital changed their story on paper as well after her death was reported. The reason they gave for not allowing her to be transferred was now a totally different story.

The night she died, they had stated Ava's problem wasn't a heart issue, so they wouldn't accept the transfer. After her death, they changed their reason, claiming that they didn't accept the transfer because there were no beds left in the cardiac unit to transfer her to. The red flags were piling up, one after the other. And no one wanted to deal with any of them. Why were there so many things that didn't add up? Why wouldn't anyone acknowledge them and investigate? This was when I went into the police station asking where they were in the investigation. This is where I was demeaned, devalued, and asked if I was making a scrapbook of Ava, with a laugh. They never investigated anything except Evan and me – why? Do you see how this question ate me alive, devoured my soul? Every parent who loses a child will ruminate on this question no matter the circumstance, no matter the cause of death.

When the question of why consumes you, it can come fast and hard, driving your every thought, every emotion. But it can also come on slowly, unnoticeable, like a gentle whisper over and over until one day you realize that it is screaming in your ear and you can't stop it, you can't hear anything else. Both ways eventually end up driving every thought, every emotion, every fear. Knowing the why is so deeply ingrained in human beings that we almost always have to know why, to be able explain it, to prove it, to right the wrong. But the truth is, sometimes the why is not for us to know in that moment in time. What if there are other things that have to happen before the big picture can come together? And what if that takes decades?

It is for us to trust that it will be discovered and unveiled in the perfect time, the perfect manner, resulting in the perfect transformation once we accept that we don't need to know why. Sometimes there is no answer to the why. Sometimes we are so busy trying to figure out why that we miss everything else, everyone else, and we just lose ourselves in it. And by the time you've lost yourself in it, you can't even see it. Because you've become it. I tried every avenue to find the why and I was met with a wall every time. But I needed to look for the reason that my child was gone. And yes, we all need to visit this visceral need to know why, it is a part of the grieving process and part of the healing process depending on the events that surrounded your child's death. There is a time for everything. The good, the bad, the joy, and the sorrow, the blame and the forgiveness. Wherever you are at in grief, know that it is exactly where you are supposed to be. It is exactly what you need, to help you shift, to help you see what you didn't see before. And there also comes a time in your quest for truth where letting go is the only way to allow the truth and the why to come forward. Sometimes the answer is right in front of you the whole time and sometimes it is the most unexpected reason that you couldn't possibly have imagined. Time is not the healer of sorrow for a child's death, but it is the pathway of things revealed, in their own perfect timing.

Finding out why this happened, the meaning behind it and the reason for my child's death, is one of the deepest and darkest wells of my grief. It was the hardest to accept. The one that consumed me, and filled me with rage, every minute of every day. It is the one thing that brought my grieving to a complete standstill. I could not make sense of the senseless. And that was not acceptable. Everything happens for a reason, but quite frankly when your child is dead, you feel that there will never ever, be a good enough reason for why they had to die.

I've always had a fight kind of response to injustices, unfairness, that familiar feeling of a rock in the middle of my chest and the innate desire to rush in and defend. I valued honesty and justice so highly at times, that it was also my downfall at other times. Even as a child, this was a familiar and strong feeling for me. And the more the lies piled up surrounding Ava's life and death and the more injustices that seemed to be happening, the more convinced I became that there was something wrong that needed to be made right. Too many things didn't add up in this story and I simply was not wired to let it go in my soul. I needed to know the truth, at all costs.

It didn't matter that there was a high probability that not one of them could have changed the outcome. This was about the truth. I needed the truth in order to process it and let it go. And I couldn't let this go without some kind of truth, reason, fairness … anything to soothe my heart. Anyone to be accountable for what has destroyed my life. I would spend months accessing every document, file, and record that I could of hers. I would pore over procedures, outcomes, heart defects, prognosis, any information that could shine a light on the truth.

As a last resort to find the truth and have people be accountable for their actions, I contacted a number of medical malpractice lawyers, even ones that were hours away. I would tell them what actually happened and all the things that weren't investigated, and the changing of stories by all these professionals. The responses varied but were all the same reasoning. Not one of them wanted to take on the police, the hospital, the doctors, and the coroner.

The truth of this situation is that you'll be bankrupted by every one of these agencies and they will say your child was sick to begin with. I'm so sorry that this is the way the system works. Do not try and take this on; I'm sorry, we can't help you with this kind of lawsuit, you're going up against major institutions. You need a lot of money and a lot of time to even consider doing this and it will be very hard on you and your other children.

Someone fight for me. Fight for my daughter. There was but one lawyer who would listen to facts and willingly agree to take this on if I thought I could handle it. *You will have the finger pointed at you for this. This is a big risk, against agencies and institutions. Their changing stories will definitely be turned around on you and they will attack you. You need to understand that the law is not about justice. There are a lot of innocent people in jail. I'm sorry, but that's the truth.* He was the last lawyer I would contact.

He was right, our justice system isn't about justice. My skin crawled at the realization of this. In my mind, the truth had the power to set me free from the why that ached in my bones. The cost of the truth was just too high, a wall so thick and so tall that I could not scale it. I could not risk my daughter losing another person in her life, first her sister, then her mother? What am I doing? Do I want to spend my life in a jail cell all because I need to know the truth about why they are lying? None of this will bring my daughter back. And no amount of money would ever be able to make me happy or fill the whole in my heart. Despair settled in, with the knowing that I would never be free.

I would never know the truth, never know why this happened. I'd never be able to piece together the puzzle, the unexplainable. I would gather everything, the notes, the records, the clothes, every little thing into a neat little pile. They all went into boxes and bins, put high up on a shelf, in the dark corner of my closet beside Ava's ashes. And there would stay my daughter, my heart, the why that would never be answered, never be honoured, and never be righted. I felt this made my heart irreparable. The loss of all systems in this world that made me feel safe, that made me believe that people were genuinely good, was a barren hole in my soul. All because I could not answer the Why. And it would eat me alive for years, deteriorating me physically, mentally, and emotionally, taking the rest of my family down with me unknowingly.

We as a society believe that we can control everything around us and the more control we have over things, places, people, situations, the better we feel, the safer we feel. That's why we ask for guarantees through marriage, through faith, through our children, through religion, through work contracts, through products, through food. We all want a guarantee. That's why we have insurance, and a system designed so that we can sue others for a wrongdoing or mistake. We all want to feel safe. We all want accountability, wrongs made right. And we are taught to use money as the means for this safety. Yet there is nothing safe about living, or being a human being. There is nothing that will keep us safe from catastrophe, betrayal, or death. Almost everyone will experience grief, a loss, a betrayal, a major setback, and every single one of us will die. No one is immune to these things, no matter how many systems we have in place or how much money we sock away or insurance we take out, all because we are taught that those are the things that make us safe. No matter how we try and fulfill our learned concepts of success it will always fall short of the fulfillment we were promised. I've lived the "successful happy life" that our world tells us should make us happy – wow, that was definitely not the happy feeling I thought it would be. Not fulfilling, not joyous, not anything worth striving for. In fact, it was the opposite. It was empty, numbing to the soul, always feeling like it was never enough. Where was the why, the purpose, the meaning? This is the world we live in. This is what we are taught from the moment we come into this world. How to be and what it will bring us if we do it right.

What if the purpose of my daughter's death was simply to show me the true meaning of life, what true love really is? To show others that death is still life. To illuminate the parts of my life that did not serve me. To uncover the lies that I believed about myself. What if her death was actually her gift to me, so that I can live fully, without fear, surrounded by love and joy? Isn't that the greatest gift someone could bestow on another? You know, I feel more joy now than I did even as a child – I've received the greatest gift from my daughter Ava – something money can't buy. Isn't that what we all are striving for – happiness and love and peace? Why do we feel that someone is always to blame? And yes, oftentimes someone is at fault. But what if they were meant to be at fault in order to bring about change? And what about those who endure abuse that strikes the most intimate parts of their soul and they rise up? Their experience fuelled their growth, allowed them to illuminate the pain and be a change maker. What if these losses and these hurts are fated to each of us in a different way and are all designed to strip away our backwards beliefs in order to free us? When I think about this, I can't help but notice that there is a change maker for every horror, every heartbreak, every exquisitely personal experience that we have, good or bad, that crushes us. There is always someone who has felt that same hurt somewhere on your road, that is desperate to know that they are not alone, that needs a light to shine on the barely noticeable path. We are all one, in life and death. Just like Pink sings, "We are billions of beautiful hearts."

But the reality is that we are frozen in fear. There was a nest of three baby birds sitting low in a Japanese maple along the countryside road at my cousin's home. She watched as the momma bird, who knew that her babies must fly if they had any chance of surviving, pushed one of the babies out of the nest. The baby was hurt from the fall and did not fly. The two babies still perched in the nest watched as their sibling died. The momma bird waited until the next day and then pushed the second baby out of the nest. This baby tried to fly with not much success other than helping it land without being hurt. The momma and this baby tweeted at each other and hopped around with delight and joy. The third baby was now sitting alone, perched in the nest and frozen with fear. Watching one sibling die and one jumping around with wonder and curiosity. He would sit for hours frozen in the state of not knowing what would happen, the fear of living and the fear of dying. We as human beings know that that tiny baby bird was unquestionably designed and meant to fly. We know that his wings were intricately made to float on the wind. That his body is perfectly proportioned and weighted to allow his wings to carry him, to cover him and protect him. But the baby bird does not know any of these things. He is paralyzed in fear of the unknown. That baby bird is me and you.

Imagine that this baby bird knew all of these things, all of these whys. He knew that he was made perfectly in every way and whichever way his first flight ended would be in perfect divine order because he would have fulfilled his own purpose and helped others find their purpose through his outcome. He wouldn't worry about why his sibling died, or whether he may have that same fate. He wouldn't question why his mother was pushing them out. He would jump with excitement and try his hand at flying, with no regret. Knowing that he was safe no matter what in the hands of Spirit, God, the Divine. Always safe, always loved in life and in death, because death is not the end of life.

If the question of why torments you, weighs you down, an incessant ache in the pit of your stomach, acknowledge it. The following is an exercise that eases the burden of why and can help you move through it. You can do this three times per week, or even once a week if you like – I did this every time my brain went back to the whys that it would replay over and over.

On a blank piece of paper write down all of your unanswered whys with no fear, no judgement of whether each why is right or wrong. Write with tears burning down your cheeks and the hole in your heart stretched wide. Feel all the anger and unfairness of it all, honour it, honour you. Once you've written your list of unanswered whys, be it one or fifty whys, fold this piece of paper up until you can fold no more. Feel the weight of it in the palm of your hand, the heaviness of those questions on your heart. I know that letting go is the hardest part for all of us. Your thoughts will scream at you in sheer rage, telling you not to let go of this anger, this burden, that you can't let go.

Know this. Letting go is what frees you and allows your child to move through you again with joy and love. You're not letting go of them, you're letting go of a painful burden that will be shown to you in time anyways. Your letting go is giving away the painful to make space for the exquisitely beautiful. The love. Sit in this for a moment. Do you want to stay sitting in this unbearable pain? Or do you want to love your child and let them love you? Love will be your answer to this every time.

If you understand this and know that you want to love your child, live with the intention of making space in your heart for your child's love. I want you to imagine now that you are giving this paper filled with all of your pain and sorrow and all of the unanswered whys to God, to Spirit, to the universe, whomever you choose. Give it to them, ask them to take care of it for you, take the burden of it from you, let them hold those questions for you. Now picture them holding this page of emotions and unanswered questions and the guilt and shame that they are covered in. Imagine that they hold these all in that piece of paper and it turns to dust and floats away in the breeze. Feel the weight lifting off your shoulders, the relief of giving the burden to Spirit. And breathe from the souls of your feet, the depths of your soul. Feel the peace of this burden that has been lifted. Feel the shift of space in your heart no matter how minuscule. Know that this is your baby filling your heart, filling you with light and love – You are making space for their love in your heart.

Chapter 5

Body, Mind, and Spirit

"Health is a state of complete harmony of the body, mind and spirit."

– BKS IYENGAR

G rieving is often concluded to be an emotional condition in our society. We're taught that it is sorrow and to try and not make the bereaved upset by talking about things. At least this is the world I lived in and how I was told of it. With absolute certainty, I can tell you without a doubt that that is the most tunnel vision, ignorant concept. Grief is all-encompassing. Body, mind, and soul. The physical effects of grief are abundant universally. And yet, these are typically ailments that a traditional western doctor cannot diagnose, other than to label it as depression and prescribe you some pills. What has our medical system come to? Scientifically, we have come light years with the greatest minds creating, experimenting, solving, and discovering at the fastest pace in human history. And yet, emotionally, spiritually, mindfully... it seems we are disconnected from the very thing that is life giving, all knowing, ever healing – our soul.

The Body, the Mind and the Heart Are Undeniably One, Both in Joy and in Pain

The first year after Ava died, I lacked the motivation to do anything and the desire for life, the light in all of our hearts, was snuffed out completely. There was no joy, no laughter, no excitement, and nothing to look forward to each day. I would wake up every morning knowing that my child was dead. The heaviness of this leaves room for little else. I had two faces. I shut down the grieving, the sadness, the unfairness, so that I could work. So that I could just make it through a day and do the bare minimum that was needed to keep my other daughter, Gabriella, and Evan going each day. There was no room for sadness, no comfort in my partners arms, no reprieve from the heaviness of despair. Each day was a silent culling of my soul, bit by bit, cell by cell. The physicalness of grief was slow to show its face. Grief is often a cross that we carry on the inside that no one sees on the outside. We are taught that this is how it should be.

My youngest child was born two years after Ava died. And it was after his birth, that I started to feel unwell. I would have odd ailments, stabbing pains, symptoms that no one could explain. By the time my son was a year and a half old, I was struggling to keep myself together. Every specialist I saw would have the same opinion:

Ms. Chandler is a lovely woman. Her case presents with an interesting constellation of non-specific symptoms. Although it does not to seem to be my specialty, it would be worthwhile to investigate other specialties to rule out any other diseases. And all but one of the eight different specialists that saw me read in my history that one of my children had died, and all recommended in their reports that I would benefit from an antidepressant. My family doctor, bless her heart, laughed at this last statement when it came in. I had been her patient since she started practicing. She was a warrior for me, persistent in sending me anywhere to figure out what was wrong with me. She knew me. I didn't go to doctors. I was always healthy prior to this. She never gave up on me and never told me I should take an antidepressant to fix it all.

It would take four years with my symptoms progressing to the point that I could barely function. Three to four days out of the week, I would get out of bed to get my kids on the school bus and then would go back to bed. Not because I was depressed. Because I was physically ill, dizziness all the time, my body stopped wanting food, it made me nauseous every time I would eat. I had the shakes, severe lethargy. My muscles were wasting away, and just vacuuming my house was so exhausting that I felt the effects of it twenty-four hours later. I would get confused, I would be angry and tired. Our medical system has a very poignant way of making people feel crazy, nuts, delusional, if you will. In fact, I had so many people that brushed me aside that I started to doubt my sanity, that maybe it was all in my head if no one could find it. We're raised with the notion that physicians are revered, prestigious in all aspects of life, knowers of all things. And you'd better believe that I used to do whatever they said, even if there was a knowing in the pit of my stomach that it wasn't right. The circumstances surrounding Ava's death had truly taught me that the role of specialists and surgeons was not to help me. They can't help you if they aren't willing to dig a bit deeper for the core of the issue. They can't help you if they only look at the physical things that show up on a scan or MRI.

Interestingly, every specialist would note something different. My body was clearly showing signs of breaking down, struggling, not functioning at the capacity it should have for a 34-year-old healthy woman. Lymphadenopathy that was getting worse, intermittent hepatomegaly with fatty tissue on it, cyanosis of the lower extremities, marked tremors, nausea, vomiting, weight loss, heart palpitations... the list goes further. But in my experience, if it wasn't blatantly obvious that there was a life and death problem or there wasn't a tumor showing on a scan or my blood work was off, but not off the charts ... Well, it's not really something they worry about.

The liver specialist was my last straw. I was referred to the liver transplant clinic with the best Hepatologist. He said they couldn't explain why I had a fatty liver considering I was so thin, and that was odd. And my blood work seemed okay, nothing off the charts. But it was the statement he made after that that was the problem, that maybe my children were stressing me out or a stressful employer was causing all the non-specific symptoms. That was the failure of a doctor to see *me* that I just couldn't take. I had a meltdown on this poor hepatologist who had no idea what was going on. I had no idea what was going on. But his appointment was my undoing. After that appointment, I gave up any desire to figure out what was wrong with me. I'd concluded that I would just let myself continue like this and slowly die, in misery and in pain. I would no longer seek a diagnosis or try to figure it out. My anger at the medical system had become as entrenched as my story, my daughter's story. I had already taken out multiple life insurance and hospitalization insurance policies through my illness, so I felt my sister would be able to financially provide for my children when my time came.

After four years of being dismissed by the medical community, an internist would finally discover what my issue was after one year of investigations with him. Postural Orthostatic Tachycardia Syndrome, otherwise known as POTS Syndrome. One entire year for proof that there was indeed a valid problem in the medical world's eyes. Proof that I was not losing my mind after four years of being dismissed. The burden this lifted from me both emotionally, mentally, and physically would allow me to manage my illness, to get better, instead of being devalued and dismissed because they couldn't physically see the problem.

The Mind Can Heal or Hurt the Body and Soul

My daughter would then guide me to see a psychologist and a few months later, I would also be diagnosed with Post Traumatic Stress Disorder, also known as PTSD, by a local psychologist. The difference between these two doctors and all the others is that they cared. They cared that I wasn't doing well. They cared that my life was in shambles. They didn't brush me aside like it was all in my head. They took things into account that most don't, they wanted to discover what the problem actually was. They were instrumental in my healing process. I cannot tell you how important it is that the people you seek help from are undeniably on your side and only want the best for you with no negativity. It is imperative to healing as a whole person.

You see, I was looking for answers to my health outside of me. Looking for the medical community to right the wrongs that had happened with my daughter.

I wanted them to make me believe in them again, to give me hope, to show me I could trust them. I couldn't see this pattern. I couldn't see anything.

Do you see the pattern repeating for me, that was a match to the ending week of my daughter's life?

The moment that it was safe, that I knew I had two people who wouldn't dismiss me, didn't make me feel like I was a burden – only then was I able to acknowledge that I hadn't grieved my daughter's death, that I hadn't accepted it, that my children were suffering, that I had no partner. Then I was able to see that my anger and grief unexpressed was eating away at my body slowly, since the day my daughter died. When I shut down my grief and stuffed the intense emotions away in a drawer because it wasn't safe, I also shut down all other emotions. Love, forgiveness, joy, sadness, empathy. All of it came to a halt. I had been operating on autopilot in danger mode for seven long years.

My body was fighting itself, because I was fighting myself. I couldn't parent my children effectively, because I couldn't accept that I failed at protecting Ava, as a parent. I couldn't help anyone else because I couldn't help myself. My grief and anger had settled into my bones and rippled through every part of my being. When I couldn't voice or feel my anger and sadness, my physical body held my spirit's emotions. They never went away, they were always there ruminating no matter how many locks were on that drawer. They seeped into my blood and my muscles. The physical illness then invaded my brain. Every thought became focused on how sick I was and how the medical system was failing me, just like it failed my daughter. These two thoughts created a reality. This would be my reality until I honoured the real problem. I required a clinical psychologist to walk me through this. Baby steps to uncover the beginning, the core, the start or cause of my dysfunction. My daughter's death. Her end was my beginning. My own body spent years telling me that my grief and anger needed to be felt. I ignored it and focused on the story, so it got bigger and bigger and bigger until my health declined to the point of total dysfunction. My mental health followed suit.

Mental Health and Grief

My mental health totally collapsed after discovering Evan had spent years lying, deceiving, and betraying me. He was the last safety net I thought I had. Key word note here is "I thought." All safety nets that we construct to live our lives are safety nets that we are taught. Your spouse, your doctor, your family, your local police, your insurance company, God. No wonder I couldn't cope mentally – all of these things that I depended on to live in safety were ripped out from under my feet. I can't tell you how terrifying it is to live in a world where there are no safety nets. Here is the thing we don't realize: living isn't safe, no matter what you concoct to feel safe by means of exterior people, institutes, or things. These actually aren't safe, there is no safety, no guarantee in life.

That is scary. What we are taught through organized religion is that God is to be feared and places judgement. Hence, the base thought, the seed that is planted in us, that grows when tragedy happens. It leads us to the questions of what did I do to deserve a life of sorrow because my child died? Or what have I done in a past life to deserve this? These thoughts come from that first little seed that we were taught by man, not by God, not by the Universe – by man alone. They set us up to feel less than, to think on an individual basis, that it's all about us. It teaches us that we are not good enough, that we need to worship and repent to someone who judges us. And that the axe will fall in our lives if something isn't done the right way. In my mind, I wasn't good enough for God, I didn't deserve to keep this child of mine, and I must have done something that caused this to happen. Everything I was taught made it harder for me to grieve and harder to accept my life and my circumstances. My mental health was directly affected by the ideas of how things were supposed to be versus how they were. This is a common place in our society and many suffer from mental health issues that stem from an upbringing or the things we were taught about the box we should be fitting into, that so many are outside of.

Mental health and grief can be a terrifying and debilitating duo. Being diagnosed with PTSD, was an eye opener on every level. The moment I started dealing with my mental health and anger and grief and disappointment and fear, was also the moment my physical health came together with my mental health. The two went hand in hand, they magnified each other's burden of trauma, of loss, of betrayal, and of a belief system that only served to enslave me in suffering. You are what you think now holds a whole new meaning. It is literally your physical body that is what you think and what you feel. When I started to see the truth in my sorrow and the lies in my beliefs, things became easier. There was suddenly a light that was shining. Sometimes it shone so brightly that I felt as light as air after having an aha moment. I started thinking and believing that I could get better. And the more I uncovered a false belief, the more I could forgive myself and the more I could open the door to forgiving others. The more beliefs I examined, the more dysfunctions of western society began to show themselves. The more I started to see all of the people in my life being held to those same beliefs and having difficulty dealing with the same issues in general, the more I recognized we are all photocopying the same beliefs of reward and punishment and needing to be absolved of our sins. If I am a child of God, this also means that my parents and their parents are children of God. Parents are the vessel to bring me here to experience life. This means I don't own my children, they aren't necessarily a reflection of me. And if I'm a child of God, then why am I responsible for my child's death? Why do I feel that it was my responsibility?

I am not God. I am a child in every aspect – learning, discovering, failing, succeeding, giving and taking, growing – we all are children, disguised in this adult concept of our society. That concept teaches us that we are responsible for life and death when we are not. It stops us from truly being who we are. Love.

The combination of my physical and mental health left me debilitated in many ways, unable to work, unable to function most days. This is what trauma and grief that is not felt and not heard can do to one's soul, manifesting into every part of their being, eating away at the person, day by day, month by month, and year after year.

The effects of poor mental health and grief combined, for my partner Evan, became more severe since we separated. The longer I was out of the relationship with Evan, the more I could see the writing on the wall and all the things about our relationship that were toxic and had helped keep me in suffering and pain, my life of misery. On my own, I was able to see the truth, and all the love and support I had never received to begin with. I don't think he ever truly mourned his daughter. He never sought out support and never wanted to talk about it.

After I ended it with him, his mental health fell apart. The result of this caused him to attack me with a barrage of blame, anger, destruction, and despair. All aimed at me. I asked his family to help him when he started to sink one year earlier, but this only incited his anger and his blaming me for his choices, his life, and his losses. I never knew if they were able to help him; they don't speak with me anymore and so I assume they weren't able to help him, because it is still ongoing. They can't help someone who doesn't want to be helped anyways. The psychologist was able to help me weed through this each week. Here I was with post-traumatic stress disorder trying to get better and receiving messages every week, blaming me, calling me every profanity in the book: "You are a horrible person and responsible for my daughter's death, you are a disgusting human being. You don't deserve children."

This is what unexpressed grief and anger mixed with existing mental health issues can result in. How do you convince someone in that state of mind that you are not the enemy? That you love them as a human being despite destroying you, that you want them to live their life and forgive themselves? How do I try and heal when faced with such anger and blame on a weekly basis?

"God Grant me the serenity to accept the things I cannot change, the courage to change the things I can, and the wisdom to know the difference."

I cannot change his actions. I can choose to recognize that his pain is great, and his words are really about himself, that his pain is masking his light, his perspective tainted by unfelt grief and poor mental health.

I often pray for him. I often send him light and love. But I cannot have a conversation with him because of his blame and anger toward me. This hurts my children more than me. They are suffering at the hands of his mental health, as they did in different ways to my own mental health.

Our Culture's Viewpoint on Death and Grief

The research and understanding of grieving a child and the short- and long-term effects on parents and siblings is minimal at best. Considering that the average number of children who die each year in the US alone, is over 50,000 children, this is a severely underserved community given the evidence of how complicated and traumatic grieving a child is. The information for bereaved parents as well as the statistics on their physical and mental health is staggeringly depressing and the ignorance of many institutions confirmed by the conclusions they came to in their studies on grief. Some of these studies and traditional models that described grief suggested that our grief should be finished two months from the date of death. More recently, some studies determined that our grief should follow the timeline of two weeks of intense grief, followed by two months of strong grief and then a slow recovery that would take about two years to complete. Various researchers also concluded that only bereaved parents who suffer from extreme emotional loneliness or severe depressive symptoms were at risk for suicidal ideation – I think anyone who loses a child, emotionally healthy or not, has the potential to be at risk simply because of the lack of support and understanding in western society.

The conclusions they came to incited me with anger at their callousness, the way they categorize and give a timeline on a subject that affects every living person and happens every minute of every day, with no two the same. Tell me, are you in the first category, where you only grieve for a few months after your child has died? Or are you in the newest, which says you have intense grief for only two weeks, followed by two months of strong grief and then all of your grief culminating slowly to an end just two years after your child has died? Do you see why our culture abandons the bereaved parent? Do you see the gigantic problem, that the lack of support, direction, and understanding of child loss is staggeringly absent? Can you imagine that our culture believes that you would only think of your sweet child who died for a few years and then are supposed to just suddenly be happy and functioning again? Which of you bereaved parents can vouch that any of that information is true? I cannot – I see through social media and grieving support groups that most parents grieve indefinitely if only because our culture does not allow us to grieve openly and our beliefs define us. Our children are not a job that we lost, or a boyfriend that broke our heart – they are often our purpose in life, our reason to do better, to smile, to give, to teach, to love – they are grown within us, a gift from God, a joy like no other and a love that knows no boundaries and no time, love that is a stronger connection than life and death. The unseen cords of pure love that energetically tie us to our children are unending, always felt, but rarely acknowledged by others who have not experienced losing a child.

This is why many of us drown in sorrow and despair – there is no space for us, no validation, no understanding. Even our employers and insurance companies do not recognize the trauma of a child dying. And yet, we buy into all of the things that they tell us are supposed to keep us safe from life's problems, illnesses, traumas, and accidents. After being off work for a year because I couldn't physically or mentally cope with life due to the trauma of unfelt grief and the betrayal, accompanied with the debilitating physical symptoms of POTS syndrome, my disability insurer would decide that none of these things should render me incapable of working. I would then be forced to fight for another year after this because my employer wouldn't allow me to come back to work after being off without the insurance company's confirmation that it was warranted. And when I did go back, they posed the question of whether I should've been off in the first place. This is just another example of how our culture denies the grief and trauma of losing a child, denies the truth that thousands of bereaved parents live every day in suffering, in pain, in despair. Our culture is designed and structured to make us feel like a burden when we ask for help, when we reveal the truth of grief. Did you know that in the eyes of some insurance companies the death of a child just isn't a traumatic enough experience to cause you to mentally not be able to go to work?

Did you know that being blamed for your child's death by both the police and your spouse is not enough to drive you to a mental breakdown? And did you know that if you aren't in immediate danger of dying in the next few months with an MRI or CAT scan or Doppler to show this, that your physical health is not considered to be 'bad' enough to warrant you not being able to go to work? These are our beliefs in this society. And I ask you, what human being could function normally and effectively in these circumstances? Not one.

When I reflect on all that has passed and all of these things combined, it still shocks me and surprises me that the world expected me to put on a happy face, a stiff upper lip and just go to work and be a standard productive member of society – and that if I didn't they would actively try to discredit me, deeming that my daughter's life wasn't valuable enough to warrant such catastrophic aftermath for me. That grief really isn't real. Sometimes I get this eerie feeling that I am being shown and experiencing all the problems that arise from grief and just how deep our misunderstanding of it goes. How dysfunctional our systems and institutions really are when it comes to grief.

Imagine how this story might be different if a space were always held for the grieving. Picture the thousands of people that have buried their children and can come to the table to live their life with meaning, purpose, and joy. This is impossible if our mental health is not supported and part of the healing process. When I imagine a place for all the grieving to come together it is like a net of love lifting every member up. The net is made from the strands of our child's love intertwined with the tears that we have shed. Because there is no place like this, I developed a retreat for healing hearts throughout the year based on this vision to bring together our broken hearts to help heal them. To bring a light to the darkness for every mother and father and show them how it feels to let go and have permission to grieve, a place where you can feel the sadness without judgement or expectation, where you are welcomed to honour this emotion. A safe place where you can connect with your child again, where peace and hope can transform your sorrow into joy and purpose. This is the kind of support that a grieving parent needs. Not a pill to put a mask on the pain.

It's so important to me that you know that sometimes lying in bed all day crying is totally normal and it is okay. *Yes,* I said this is okay, no guilt allowed. You are supposed to feel that way; you have just buried your child, your hopes, your dreams, your dream job – called motherhood –one of the biggest purposes in your life. Do not rush your mourning. There is no timeline, no deadline you have to meet. You don't need anyone to give you permission to grieve when it hits you out of nowhere. You don't need people to tell you that you need to control it or should be over it. Know deep in your heart that your love was so deep that the sorrow will match it. Give yourself permission to never have to paste a smile on your face for others because they are uncomfortable. Remember that you can feel angry and scream and shout, letting all of these real emotions that we feel, have a breath of air. When you illuminate that darkness, that rage, it becomes honoured and allowed to be. This also allows it to turn to dust and leave your heart. Surround yourself with people who can talk about your child, or simply sit with you in the sorrow. Don't bury these feelings like I did. They will sink into your very being, ripple through your muscles, and invade every thought you have. That is not what your child wants. They want to hold you while you cry, knowing that you have truly experienced the power of selfless true love at the very core of its essence. They want you to sit in the discomfort and in the unpleasant intensity of grieving. Do you know why? Because your joy, your love, and your real life is waiting for you on the other side of it, but you've got to feel all of it and walk through it to get there. Don't let anyone discredit or disvalue how you feel, don't let anyone else's discomfort make you feel that you cannot talk about it. Speak your truth, in all of its glorious pain and dysfunction.

Everything is possible when we choose to love that uncomfortableness of grief.

Chapter 6

Relationships

"You learn more about someone at the end of a relationship than you do at the beginning."

– Unknown

Every relationship you have is forever altered after the death of a child. Your spouse, your children, your friends, your family, your co-workers, and most importantly, your relationship with yourself. I found that I would be unable to function one day and when I was able to move around, Evan was not functioning at all. It would go back and forth between us. Gabriella, my oldest daughter, and I would have moments of joy and moments of quiet sorrow, at opposite times and at the most inopportune times. I could no longer be near my friends or my sister, for they were all having babies and I had just buried mine. No one grieves the same way or in the same order. We are all intrinsically designed to experience death and loss, and yet no two losses are the same, no grieving is the same, and every heart is shattered in different patterns. There are so many boxes to fit into and yet only a handful will fit into each box when it comes to grief. After Ava died, many people in my life fell by the wayside. They either stopped contacting me, or when they did make an effort to support me, I couldn't respond to them. I couldn't function long enough to put any effort toward anything. At the end of it all, only my family and two friends from childhood remained after this tragedy. And in hindsight, these were the best people that would stand by me for eight years watching me wither away and still did not let go, did not give up on me. They didn't know how to help me and I didn't know what I needed to help me either – but these people would stand with me despite not knowing how to fix it. Don't worry about the people that fall away from you in your grief. They know that they aren't able to provide what you need if they can't hold space for your pain. So let them fall away from you.

Friends and Family

What many don't realize is that the death of a child is followed by the death of many relationships with friends and family. The burden of sorrow is often too heavy to hold anything that is not rooted in the deepest respect and love. The people you lose are often blessings in disguise, a shedding of things and opinions and people that no longer serve you – that cannot help you. Take heart, there will be but a few that shine and linger in the dark with you, no matter how much time has passed, no matter how your pain hurts them too – these are the ones you are meant to uncover in the shedding. Then there are the ones that are souls intertwined with yours, that walk in when the rest of the world walks out. That even when they have no idea how to help you, they will patiently wait, silently pondering and helping without your knowledge.

My daughter's death didn't just affect me, the grief would stagnate other relationships, stopping them from blooming, affecting others' lives as well. My sister and I were pregnant together, due dates one month apart. I cherished this for so many reasons. I believed that our girls would grow up together and be the best of friends, just as my sister and I were now. I was there for my niece's birth in May and so grateful to be in that room to see the emotion, the rawness, the immediate joy when that baby girl let out her first wail. I was there to welcome this little angel into the world. I loved my niece Sophia, the moment I set eyes on her. I mean loved as if she were my own, as if she was a physical part of me. But, after Ava died, I couldn't be around Sophia for the better part of a year. Every milestone she would hit, I knew would be a milestone I would never experience with Ava. It hurt so badly that I just couldn't bear to be a part of my sister's joy. An entire year of both my sister's firsts as a new mother and my niece's year of firsts. Everything that I had been so excited about, the anticipation of them when we were pregnant, the amazing opportunity to share one more connection in life with my sister, and I would miss them all that first year. Just one more loss of something in my life since my daughter died, and these differ for everyone. Watching other mothers consumed and elated with love for this little human being that was their gift was at times excruciating to watch without becoming angry. Why do they still have their child? Or why does someone who doesn't want children, or abuses children, still get to have their children for life? Why do they deserve it and I don't? It was hard to find joy in other people's children when it was a reminder of the crushing loss of my daughter, the hole in my heart that I simply could not fix. I hated this fact, hated the other mothers, and then I hated myself for feeling like I was not worthy in the eyes of God to keep my little girl. And then I hated myself for thinking these things about people.

My mother would struggle too, feeling helpless in how to help me, but tried in everyway to do it. She made every effort to include us in every holiday to make sure that we attended, that we were surrounded by family. In one moment she would hold me while I cried and in the next she would be frustrated that I just wasn't thriving, wasn't moving – stagnated and drowning in unfelt grief. She would be enraged at the medical doctors as she watched me grow sicker and sicker. I suspect that the role of a grandparent is difficult because they are grieving their grandchild but are also grieving for their own child's loss. They are helpless in not being able to fix it. A mother feels all her children's excitement, disappointments, successes, and failures. My mother would now be experiencing my grief and my failing health. She would ride the emotional roller coaster with me, but with a different viewpoint, a different belief and feelings. The role of a Mother is forever, unending, through thick and thin, joy and pain. This is the beauty of the Mother and the cross that she bares.

The relationships affected didn't stop there - Only a few lifelong friends would commit to waiting with patience for me and who truly understood the depth of my loss, even when I could not speak with them or see them – even when it spanned years, they would wait for me. Two childhood friends would lie in wait, Dani and Jeannie. After two years that I disappeared from their lives after Ava died. Jeannie called me one day out of nowhere, asking without judgement, without fear, and with love filling every word she spoke, "I don't know if I fit in your life since Ava died. I'm wanting to know if I still fit in your life, if I should keep trying, if you want me to keep trying. It's okay if you don't, but I need to know. I love you and I want to keep trying if you want me to." These words lit a candle in the darkness of my heart. They gave me hope that I could trust in someone who truly wanted what was best for me, that I had not been abandoned completely. It was a sudden understanding that those who are willing to wait for me are those that are worthy of all my love, all my heart, and all my soul. Jeannie is the sort of friend we all dream of and imagine with joy in our hearts at having someone who loves us and wants what is best for us, without dictating it, without deciding how we should be. She is my cheerleader to become who I was meant to be. She sees all of the good in me and shines her light on it. "You can do this. Think how far you've come, all that you have been through. You can do this." Her words of encouragement throughout my life have always come at the moments that I felt I couldn't keep going. She would remind me of who I was, my strength, my soul. When I got lost and couldn't remember myself, she would be my reminder. When I felt weak, she named my strength. When I felt not one more step could be made, she reminded me that the path of truth was waiting for me. This is the kind of person that you need to surround you, to hold your heart in the vulnerable state of grief. Look for ones that judge not, but instead encourage. The ones who listen without opinions. They have stepped into your path for a reason. Let them love you.

In the aftermath of my breaking free from Evan, there would be a select few others who could not span those years with me after Ava died but would come full circle to open their arms to me again, seven years later. My dear friend Marissa, whom I hadn't spoken to since Ava's death, welcomed me with open arms and heart, right back into her life, without hesitation. I asked for a sign that I could reach out to her and I received it hours later. A post with a call to support her photography business, just after I'd also asked for a sign to help me find a professional photographer. I had no idea that that was her craft or that she even liked photography. Ask and you shall receive – this was my confirmation to reconnect with her and intertwine her life with mine again. She never once blamed me, never stopped thinking about me, and never judged me that I didn't and couldn't connect with her for all these years. Even when I detailed the destruction and dysfunction that came after Ava died, she was ready to listen. A true friend that falls away because you are paralyzed with grief and aren't able to reciprocate or give energy to, will do exactly as Marissa has done. She knew that there was nothing she could do, she said that she worried that maybe she had done something to upset me. Those that are part of your life and can share meaning and purpose will come back to you with nothing but love when you let them go. The gratitude I feel knowing that I have people like this in my life often brings me to tears. I am so blessed and in awe of how we truly always get what we need, when we need it, even if we can't see the forest through the trees.

Children and Grief

The first month after Ava died, people had lots of statements that were directive of their expectation of Evan and me, and even of Gabriella, who was six when her sister died. I'm blessed to have her in my life. Gabriella is an old soul and can light up a room with her smile. She was so excited to have a little sister – it didn't phase her one bit that her sister had heart surgery. To her this was totally normal. She didn't question it, didn't worry about it, she just danced and sang around her, made videos of her new addition to our family. These are the only videos that I have of my daughter Ava. I was too wrapped up in the care and the worry and all the things I needed to do for her every day to even think about taking home videos. I'm deeply grateful that Gabriella was present in the moment with the innocence and joy of a child, she revelled in those moments. And I regret not cherishing them like she did. If only I had known they would be so short and bittersweet.

Seven years after her sister's death, Gabriella finally opened up about Ava's death and some of her perspective. Interestingly, this coincided with my being able to finally grieve Ava. Giving myself permission to grieve would finally give Gabriella the permission to grieve her sister as well. At her sister's funeral, she was told that she needed to take care of her mom and her stepdad now that Ava was gone. She was told that Evan needed a daughter. Evan is not her paternal father but had been with us since Gabriella was three years old, and she loved him deeply, idolized him even. My six-year-old daughter did exactly what she was told and sat on his lap and told him that it was okay, he could be her Daddy and she loved him. Imagine being six years old and the statement of looking after her parents was what she took to heart and remembered deep in her soul of that experience. This little girl is the epitome of love, giving, and kindness, mixed with despair and anger at life and all that she has lost. Her life as a fourteen-year-old now has been fraught with the perils of relationships, loss, negativity, and being alone. They say that the death of a child is the most difficult for a sibling because they are losing more than anyone. They lose the sibling that would be or is the only person in the world that will experience their family in a similar role, under their parents. But they also lose their parents in that loss too, both emotionally and mentally as the parent's grief is so intense. They lose both. I did not do a very good job at parenting after Ava's death. I was so deeply affected I couldn't handle it, I couldn't handle parenting when my six-year-old would be off playing and laughing and want to do something with me. I just couldn't do it, it hurt too much. It is normal for children to ask questions and laugh and play. They process death differently than we do. They also are deeply connected to the universe, God, and Spirit. They are not burdened yet with all the rules and boxes that they will be shamed into fitting into as they get older. My inability to cope deeply affected her, and all the things that we would lose in the years after would start to layer the burdens and hard things in life on top of her. I see in her all these burdens covering her light, all the hurt bubbling in her chest and the words that she spits out when her heart is aching. When I look back at this, I feel such shame in not being able to help her, to do right by her. But here is the truth in this. I did the best I could, even though my best was nowhere close to what it should have been. I was a product of the things I was taught and didn't question. I was grappling with life after one of my children had died. It took many sessions and many tears to forgive myself for failing her in this regard. I had to see and know without a doubt that I too am a child of God like her. Gabriella is a child of God, not mine. The famous poet, Khalil Gibran, puts the truth of our children in perspective, "Your children are not your children. They are the sons and daughters of Life's longing for itself. They came through you but not from you and though they are with you yet they belong not to you." There is a sigh of relief in this truth in the depths of my soul. Let it resonate with you as well, for it shines a whole new light on this role of a parent. I see now that Gabriella's journey through life will result in strength and compassion, a resiliency and love and light that will shine again when she can face it all, knowing that she is safe to be who she truly is – Love. The better I have gotten at processing the truth of death and our lives, the better she has been able to slowly let the pain trickle out. It is the recognition that my job as a parent isn't to tell her what she should or shouldn't do or how to feel, but rather to allow her to experience her life how she needs to, to learn the lessons this life has for her. She will undoubtedly surpass my generation's capability of living in the moment and loving with all her heart with no regrets. Little by little she is seeing that she is safe to be herself, to speak, to feel, to love despite hurt. Uncovering her layers of beauty has been a treasure of joy. I am forever grateful for her love and forgiveness of my shortcomings as a parent. She has been my teacher. Children have so much to teach us about life and death and living in the moment. They are really teaching us to remember what life is all about. Gabriella is teaching me in life and Ava is teaching me in death. I am truly blessed, given two gifts that are on complete opposite sides of the spectrum, gifts of immeasurable abundance, growth, and love.

My son, Domenic, was born two years after Ava's death. The desire to have another child after Ava was a deep visceral need that was so great that I knew within a month of her death that I wanted another child. Interestingly, I had renounced my desire to have any more children once we were discharged from the children's hospital with Ava. I knew it was too much to have a child who would possibly need to undergo multiple heart surgeries as she grew and then have more children. I'm forever grateful that I didn't enforce that lack of desire to have more children by getting a hysterectomy.

This is when people bring up the concept of the replacement child. This is a term that is grossly misplaced and mislabelled. I wasn't looking to replace my daughter. Nothing could replace her or fill that hole in my heart. I wanted another child for another chance to love like a mother loves a newborn child, to be a better mother, to love them even more, to have hope again, to live again, to feel the joy of bringing that little person grown inside me for nine months into this world. Maybe those are the wrong reasons to have another child after her death, but maybe they are all the right reasons. Having a child after the death of another child was the most basic need that had to be met in my heart. It was also tainted with the fear that something may go wrong. I knew I would never come back from losing another child, or feel the despair and sorrow twice over. Once my son was born I would continue to feel that fear, that sense of no control over life and death. I was meticulous at watching Domenic's every movement, every reaction, if he met every milestone. The fear of his dying was like a swirling black cloud that haunted me day and night. It was a seed that incubated in the back of my mind, clouding every decision I made. Life is different when you have experienced every parent's worst fear. You now know that life can be destroyed in a matter of moments and you also know the dust choked desert that lays beyond it. And you will do anything to prevent that tragedy from repeating itself again. This is part of the truth of life after losing a child – you now fully understand that you have no control. No matter how meticulous, how caring, how loving, how strategic or persistent you are – you don't get to decide whether your child lives or dies. You can turn your back for one second and your life has changed.

I spent Domenic's first four years of his life in the grip of this fear and he too learned to exist in the invisible grips of my fear. I could see it spilling over into his reactions and discoveries – they too were laced with fear. With my fear. Not his. But mine. All because I could not see that I was not God; not the decider of fates. Once I could fully accept my daughter's death without blaming myself for not knowing and not being able to save her, that was a turning point. This realization brought peace to my soul. It allowed me to let the universe look after those things that I could not control. It was a losing battle, that we are all doomed to fail at. I was the keeper of my own suffering and could not see through the trees for what it was. Since recognizing the beauty of allowing the universe to hold me, I could then let the universe hold my children, too. I could turn my back once more to get them a drink from the kitchen and know deep in my soul that the universe has got this. The universe has me and my children. It allows you to breathe again, to move about without tiptoeing through the broken glass that the floor of 'what if' is covered in. It allows freedom in your movements, and your thoughts. And when these moments of fear happened as I watched my children, I was able to sit in that feeling where your chest is boarded down, breath caught in your throat and heart pounding. I could see it without judgement, from outside of it. Slowly I could let the air out of my chest and imagine the hands of universe holding them. "They are okay. I am okay. Breathe." I would repeat this to myself three times. And the fear and rigidness would pass. And then I could breathe again, my body would relax again. I started off only catching myself doing this once or twice a week. But the more I was aware that these feelings were happening, I was able to catch myself in the panic, in the fear of loss and smooth it out, conciously rewrite it in my thoughts. This simple exercise practiced over and over, slowly through the last year has rewarded me greatly. More importantly, my living children are flourishing in their own experience of not having to be afraid since I've implemented this change. They have permission in their hearts to test the waters without fearing every drop of water that lands on them. Sometimes they and I revert back to our old thinking and feelings, that's normal. We simply reevalute and readjust and remember why fear is not who we are.

I think all parents have their own fears that stem from their unique experiences and we can't help but try to instil the fear in our children because it is so real to us. Some children take that fear as their own and it grows with them, while other children balk at it and push it away with a knowing that it is not theirs, the need to experience is far greater than the fear for some of them. You never know which of these paths a child will grow into. They are their own person, again a child of God, a spirit so unique that there is no one in the world like them. The simple act of grieving my daughter and acknowledging the fear that had become me, allowed me to dismantle it piece by piece, peeling back the layers of fear and lies. The truth is, we do not control life and death, but we seem to think that we do, looking for someone or something to be responsible for life and death. But we simply cannot control other people, it is literally impossible, other than physically shackling them. It requires two people in agreement of one controlling and the other submitting. Often, we simply fall into this pattern, or fight to feel we are controlling the other person, the outcome. This is a fight we will never win. We do not possess other people. I do not possess my children, rather I'm holding a space for them to experience life on their own terms. Their own spirit is free and wild and will live the life they were meant to no matter how hard I try to control it. I do not get to decide who stays and goes and how long they are here. They do. And they do it for a reason whether we feel it is senseless or not. Relinquishing control and the burden of feeling that I was responsible for what happens to my children on the grand scale of things was like a thousand bricks being lifted off of me. Light as a feather and able to see a broader perspective when I let this go.

One of Ava's gifts to me was Domenic and I'm grateful for my son every day. When I was pregnant with Gabriella in

2003, a woman told my mother that my daughter was bringing down a boy, then she hesitated and said that it actually wasn't this daughter I was pregnant with that was bringing me a boy, it was another daughter. Then in 2012, when I was pregnant with Domenic, again another woman told my mother that my daughter was bringing me a son and to let go of the worry. There was nothing to worry about it. These two women gave the exact same words through the same messenger, my mother, that my daughter would bring me a son, exactly eight years apart. There is a bittersweetness to those premonitions for me, a comfort in the understanding that this was meant to be part of my story and a grander purpose for the sadness. That there are no mistakes, no matter how painful or loving, despite the experience being disgusting or beautiful, they are all right, for you and them in each moment.

Spouses and Grief

About a month after Ava's death, I remember poignantly Evan's closest friend saying to me that Evan and I would always be together after going through the death of our child together. It's interesting because I had two opposite internal reactions to that statement. I shuddered and felt trapped first and then the opposite end of the spectrum, slowly came a feeling of safety after experiencing the fallout of so many safety nets surrounding her death. Looking back, the first reaction was my intuition trying to guide me and the second reaction was the seeds of society's carefully laid agenda for what was and wasn't safe or successful.

The truth is that the death of a child can only go in one of two ways. It can open you up to all the hurt and pain and vulnerability to comfort you and solidify that relationship, making it unequivocally whole, safe, and loving between the two of you. *Or*, it can be the great divide between two people who no longer recognize who they are or any semblance of the life they had planned. That friend's comment became my own thought, despite my intuition pushing back on it. I would hold tightly to that and thought that we were in the first category of solidifying the relationship and that it would deepen our roots and spread wings in my heart. But that never happened, and I was so burdened with unexpressed grief that I couldn't open up because it wasn't safe with him either. For seven years I went about my days in my own thoughts and emotions, rarely speaking of Ava and how I felt. Instead I focused on the outer world, the world that was measured by things, acquisitions. The expectation of society's idealism of success is grossly incorrect, in fact the opposite of what each of us should strive for. I followed all the rules after Ava's death, hoping that it would bring me to peace – get the bigger house, the better car, the higher income, the facade that we were a perfect happy family – after all, this is how Evan viewed success and happiness and the trap of not having enough that he lived in. The material world that I was living in was not part of my value system, it did not fill the giant hole in my heart. I've lived that ideal successful happy life that our society tells us should make us happy. Guess what, I was not happy at all. I was unfulfilled, with a serious lack in every area of my life. I chose the exterior things to fill my broken heart and when I achieved the exterior things, my heart was still broken and I realized that I didn't want any of it. It changed nothing. The proposed societal measures of success and fulfillment was a lie.

Just when I thought nothing could be worse in life and I just needed to get through each day, I discovered by accident Evan's infidelities, both physical ones and emotional ones. And I would later discover that it had spanned a large chunk of the years following our daughter's death. This didn't just crush me, it broke me wide open. And all the grief I had hidden deep down spilled out uncontrollably. Along with the rage, the tears, the unfairness of life, the acknowledgment that the last hanging strand in the web of my life had given way. There is a saying that the only thing worse than a partner cheating is the death of a child. When I read this on a psychologist's website, I came undone. God … what had I done to deserve these things that no one ever wants to experience? How pathetic am I to be living in this giant web of lies, a life that was never real, never whole, and filled with anguish? Who am I?

Here was the person that I had held with shared tears as we watched our daughter being cremated. Ashes to ashes, dust to dust. Did that mean nothing? He didn't just betray and devalue me in all ways, he had just devalued the life and death of our daughter and all that we had gone through. His actions devalued our whole life, the lives of his son and stepdaughter. Clearly, Evan had a different perspective, that it was my fault. An apology was always followed with a but. He felt I was responsible for fixing his mistakes and the onus of all laid on me. As it always had. I was sick, trying to work full time, doing everything for the kids from the moment they woke up to when they went to sleep, picking up after his alcoholic father who was living in my house – and, for the cherry on top, I paid for almost everything in our life together.

His response to this was, "I knew you were suffering and failing and I knew what you needed to help you. I just chose not to help you." This was so painful, so specific. This was the only person in the world that loved and lost in the same experience as me, telling me that not only was I not valuable, but that I wasn't even worth helping when I was drowning. That it was okay to watch me wither away, watch me suffer, knowing that he could make a difference but chose not to because I wasn't worth it. And yet, one of his alcoholic girlfriend's on the side seemed to be more worthy than I, as he had openly tried everything to get her help, as a friend, while watching me drown. Knowing that I needed help, knowing that our children were suffering emotionally with this as well. His actions and words clearly showed me that I was not worthy to him, nor were his children worthy to him. We all suffered.

And so his plight continued as he blamed me for all that was wrong in his life and all of his actions. He had held me responsible for his happiness as a human being. No wonder I failed, no one in the world could succeed at being responsible for someone else's happiness. Two weeks before discovering his latest betrayal, I remember lying in bed at night, alone and feeling so small and filled with rage. I thought to myself, I have to stay with him until he dies, I can't leave the person I buried my child with. I had believed someone else's expectation of how my relationship should continue and made them my own trap without even being aware of it. The stories and truths that he would later disclose to me were shocking and paralyzing for me. Frozen in the recognition that his mental health issues went far deeper than I had thought or seen. That I had no idea who this person was and that this person held none of the values that are at my core, as a human being, as a soul. Many say that you cannot know what you do want unless you have experienced what you don't want. And out of the experience of what you don't want comes the honing and direction toward what you do want. This would prove true as it uncovered how little I had valued myself. My daughter's death was not intended to make me suffer, nor a punishment for any action I had taken in the past. But rather, it was to allow me to see through the lens of Spirit, to see who I truly was, to break everything down until every truth was laid before me – so that I could rebuild and construct a life of self-love, joy, and self-empowerment. But instead of seeing that, my grief, anger and shame took hold of my mind and I delved further into powerlessness, with my taught beliefs directing me rather than my soul guiding me. I needed Evan to break all of it even more, in order for me to be free. I could tell you that I could've learned an easier way without the pain, but clearly that was not the case. Ava's death was meant to show me the truth about myself, the power of relationships between people, to uncover the facade that was my life. Just as Evan was meant to help me destroy the idea and beliefs of unworthiness that I had of myself so that I could find my true self and worth. I am grateful to him for the role he has played in my life, for this breaking of my world and for helping me bring Ava and Domenic into my world.

Unfortunately, my oldest daughter Gabriella would not go unscathed by Evan's inability to be accountable for himself and his actions. She was deeply hurt by him; as he continued his attack on me, he secretly doubled up the blame on her. He would tell her that it was her fault that I was sick, because she didn't help enough. And that it was her fault that he did what he did, because she didn't love him enough. He told her that she would not be able to function without him and her life would be awful, that she'd never do anything. Here is my first true love of my life, my thirteen-year-old daughter, being manipulated, cut down, and blamed by the father figure that she loved so dearly for things she could never control. This broke my heart as much as his betrayal. These are the layers of hurt that are a result of mental health and grief that is not dealt with, coupled with narcissistic qualities that I had allowed to manipulate me for years because I was so broken from my daughter's death. In allowing Evan to manipulate me through those years, I unknowingly showed Gabriella that it was okay to be treated that way, that it was okay for someone to manipulate, devalue and discredit her. I had to lay down all of my hurt and anger and shame for her. Then I had to show her that our life was not okay, not normal, and not the loving home that we deserved. The courage to end this relationship with Evan would take three months and after that was a constant assault on my integrity as a person, verbal abuse and him using my son as a pawn for alienation.

I ended up feeling that my home wasn't safe anymore, as Evan had a key and when he came to take the remainder of his things, he also took everything we had of Ava. Every memento, every card, every piece of clothing, every picture, and all of her medical records. This crushed me and I wept on the floor of the basement, sobbing, feeling that I had nothing left of my baby girl. There were no clothes that smelled like her anymore, no picture that I could brush my hand across lovingly and remember her face. No ashes, the last of her body to bury or keep, I hadn't decided. I spent hours on the basement floor that day. It was one thing to destroy me and our relationship, but it was another to take everything we had of our daughter Ava – to strip me of the one thing I could never replace, and he knew this when he did it.

Evan also took Domenic's birth certificate and demanded that Domenic get a passport right away. He said he was leaving for Japan to marry a Japanese woman who was pregnant with his child, and that he wanted his son to go with him. At first I thought this was wonderful that he was getting married, it meant that he was moving on and would be too busy to harass me and would leave me alone. A mixture of relief for myself and empathy for his new wife was felt through out me. However, with such unstable behaviour and the anger Evan clearly displayed toward me, I had to draw the line, set a boundary to protect my children's emotional and mental health. Disallowing Domenic to be used as a pawn. I couldn't allow my son to be put in this situation with such erratic and manic depressive behaviour and yet it broke my heart to have to make that decision. Everyone should be allowed to see their children, but not if it hurts the child more than it helps. Evan refused to discuss separation and custody even when this was the only avenue to see his son. Both my lawyer and I tried to reason with him, but you cannot reason with someone who is unreasonable, irrational. Things would escalate to Evan verbally attacking me on a daily basis, progressing to following me. The inclusion of the police in the matter only served to incite more anger directed at me. Evan was enraged, like he was a victim and I was the perpetrator of all the things wrong in his life. I remember vividly the strong hold of that feeling, of being a victim at the hands of someone else, like life is happening to you instead of for you and from you. But it is only a perspective, a choice to see it that way, a thought that you tell yourself...but does it make it true? Evan is not a victim, he is creating his own life through his actions and words. I too went through a shift in perspective of my part in my own previous beliefs that I believed I was a victim. Bereaved parents feel like a victim in a monumental way – Their child is dead – Nothing is more confirming of the feeling that life is happening to you, than this circumstance. It takes honesty and courage and openness to relinquish that feeling, to cast it out of your existence. The freedom in doing so allows you to take flight, banishes the shadows of doubts, illuminates the power that each of us has within.

Clearly the effects on both Evan and I, and our relationship after Ava's death, had a ripple effect that ran deep through both of us, for so many years, that the breaking of our hearts and our relationship was a mental breakdown for him and myself in our own ways. The difference between Evan and I, is that I got help and I genuinely wanted to get better, to feel better, to live, to be happy – whereas Evan did not get help and would refuse to acknowledge he needed it, clearly enjoying the misery that he lived in, choosing to stay in the victim and blaming mentality that he would barrage me with thereafter. This makes me feel so sad for him, knowing that he is choosing to stay in that kind of pain and suffering.

I want to be really clear that this is my story alone and most marriages do not end like mine did after the death of a child. Yes, there will be some of you reading this, knowing that parts of my story are truths in your story. And yes, the statistics show that most marriages do not survive the death of a child. But there are relationships that grow and evolve, deeply connected by the loss of their child such that their marriage reaches a whole new level of deep love and compassion for each other. I have seen this and I know it is possible, but it takes honesty, respect, and love that was there to begin with. The death of a child is a make or break for every marriage or relationship you have. The casualties of your life that follow the death of a child are many and they run as deep as the blackest parts of the ocean and as wide as the universe. Most people only see that you lost a child and do not understand it, when the truth is that your child's death was the biggest blow to your soul, and that many secondary losses follow it – your entire life and all that you were is on the line. No one talks about the small deaths of your life that seem to pile on afterwards.

Sometimes I recognize that Ava's death was the bringer of truth about my relationships with men, with family, and with myself and Spirit – It was a wake up call alerting me that it was merely the heavily prolonged end of a relationship that died when my daughter had died. That I had clung to with fear and sorrow. Fear has many faces and can lead us to making choices that we would never make otherwise, that our soul is trying to lead us away from. Learn from joy or pain. Sometimes we bring it on ourselves and sometimes it comes out of nowhere and you're there whether you want to be or not.

Change can be hard. It can feel like a mountain when you're trying to put a whole different program for your lives into play, not just for me, but for both my children, each in their own way. This is the same as grieving a child. Except you suddenly have a whole new life program that started playing without you, and it's a program of loss, one you didn't choose. This program is like a storm that sweeps in and leaves destruction in its wake and you're completely lost without the life program you signed up for, expected, and planned for. You're left to wonder who picked this crappy, awful program and what happened to the wonderful joyful one you thought you had picked out? When you've lost all faculties and you're trying to claw your way to the rewind button so you can get back to the program that it was supposed to be, the life you had planned for and all the joy and memories you would share with your child. Stop looking for the rewind button. It isn't there. Instead there is a gift disguised as despair.

There are so many gifts in the relationships that change after the death of a child. Even the ones that burn more holes in your heart. The key is letting go. Be the painful mess that you truly are and acknowledge all the awful feelings and changes that come after your child's death. Let your pain show, give your heart a voice, hold your grief up and honour it for all it is. As a couple, this is how you grow together, grieve together, and strengthen each other. You cannot predict or control your grief, let alone your partner's or your children's. Letting go is the hardest thing to do when every instinct you have is telling you to hold tightly.

Again, I'm grateful for Evan's inability to love me or help me in the way I needed. He set me free, really shone the light on how I did not value myself, how I allowed someone else to dictate how I felt. This second disaster of shock and pain would again come as a surprise that I did not see coming, that I could not control. The death of a child will most certainly break open all wounds for both you and your spouse, the good and bad, the truth – let the breaking continue and you will rise together or see that there is something greater for you when you move forward on your own. Know that it doesn't matter which of these is your path because there is no right or wrong path to take. Sometimes all doors lead to the same truth, some are just longer than others. Evan was the bringer of my freedom door that would appear unexpectedly for me to walk through and finally grieve and honour my daughter. This was a door of many freeing points – a door to close on those that were only serving themselves and destroying me in the process. A door that gently hung ajar, beckoning me to see who I truly was and what my value was. When I stepped through that door and truly faced the pain of it all, I learned that I decide how people are allowed to treat me. That I am intensely loyal and giving to the very end. That I am forgiving in the face of pain. I am beautifully broken and so much more than what others told me I was. I've learned that the people who never left my side no matter how much I isolated myself are the true givers and healers and a solid testament to the power of supporting in unification, to the power of souls connecting out of love. I learned that I am not just me, I am you and him and her and Spirit, I am all of you and you are all of me.

I would encourage you to walk through that door. Walk through it with your heart in pieces when your tears have run dry. You will never regret it, it will pull you and your spouse together with love, or let go with love. Your door is there for a reason. And it's waiting for you to walk through it.

Chapter 7

The Spirit of Ava

"For life and death are one,
even as the river and the sea are one."
– KHALIL GIBRAN, *THE PROPHET*

I f there is one major thing that the death of a child makes you question, it is exactly that – death. What happens? Is it the end and if so, how can that be the end? Is God real and are they with God in this utopian Heaven that we have been taught about? And what about Hell and baptism and all the 'requirements' to be in heaven? And do those requirements even exist if it is a child? I could write you a thousand questions that I asked myself more than once, trying to understand the inexplainable. Trying to place my daughter's existence after death into the neat little packages that I was taught. She never fit in them. None of our taught religions make sense when you are in the thick of the loss of a child.

There is no reasoning, no explanation that fit. I would shut down from everything, because the life and love and process that I thought life was, in fact, was actually based on all that I had been taught by religion, by society, by my experiences. They all led to shame, despair, and unhappiness.

I will never forget the feeling of first knowing that my daughter was all around me, walking with me, trying so hard to connect with me. The refuge and undeniable softening of my heart was palpable in every muscle, every thought, every heartbeat. Her truths would tell me my truth. Her acknowledgement of me and mine of her would set in motion miracle after miracle, healing and wholeness, purpose and direction. But above all, the feeling of divine, Godly love that resonated deep within me, an affinity for all living things that too were love. The connectedness of life, that coincidences were simply not coincidences, but divinely timed signals, pathways, acknowledgements of you and the power you hold and the symbol of infinity.

Before I started writing today, a hummingbird grazed my ear and then hovered not three inches in front of my face. I knew I was about to tell you my truth, Ava's truth about death, that it is nothing that secular religions teach. You and I are forever, unending in energy, Spirit, and connectedness. The symbolism of this earthly but magical creature gracing me with its presence before I tell you this truth, is that their wings fly in the infinity symbol pattern, the never-ending connection of life, of death, of energy, of Spirit, of you and me.

Jade is an extended family member that I did not interact with very often. I've known her for twenty-five years, and yet never knew her as a person, never had a meaningful conversation, never exchanged events from daily life at all. Little did she or I know that she would be the messenger of spirits and a hero in my life. She would bring the truth to light, the hurt to heal and the despair to hope. She was frank and vulnerable at her newly rediscovered gift. "This is all a bit crazy, yes, I have been getting messages from Spirit, people who have passed. Very few people know. It sounds so crazy but I don't like saying I talk to people who have died. They, Spirit, are so alive, it feels like I am just talking to someone on the phone." Jade too, was grappling with the confines of what we are taught is normal or acceptable. She too is walking the edge of the wall society has built around us, wavering between the truth of the unknown in her heart and the confines of safety and fear that we live every day. Jade was willing to sit in the uncomfortableness, the unexplainable, and the judgement of mainstream society's ignorance and perspective on the Spirit side of life. And she was doing it for me. My gratitude for her courage to step outside this box to help me, is unending, forever burned in my heart and soul that we can give to those in pain the gift of relief, redemption, healing, and love. There is nothing I could give her that would measure up to the gift she would give me next. She was instrumental in reconnecting me to myself and to my daughter Ava. The tragic love story of a mother and daughter would come full circle, to be realized as a poetic love story that spanned mountains of inner turmoil and lies to see the truth.

Do you remember when I told you that I was yelling in my head *I give up!?* This was when the hepatologist dismissed me, this was also just days after I ended the relationship with Evan. I was completely broken, in every way that a person can be. My moment of surrender was Ava's moment to take the reins, and my Grandmother June's way to make sure that I made the connection. Jade would come out of nowhere, as if by magic, after I gave up, to tell me my every thought, every sorrow, every hurt. "Your daughter Ava and your Grandmother June are coming to me. Most times Ava comes to me she makes me cry, I can feel her emotions. She's telling me that you need a message right away. They're saying you gave up."

This would stop me in tracks. My heart felt like it had stopped and time had slowed to nothing. *I did give up. Just days ago I gave up,* I thought. I had told no one that I gave up, except myself.

Jade continued, "I've written down the things they've been saying to me over the last few weeks for you. Erin has a lot of grief and anger. Dealing with it and seeing a psychologist will help alleviate health problems. Grief and anger have manifested in her body from not releasing the emotions. Ava is with her, June, your Grandma, and in good hands. Live life now. There will be a time you'll be with her, Ava, again." Jade knew nothing of my health issues, the betrayal of my partner, the struggles I had been drowning in. In fact, Jade's recount of Spirit's message for me about my health is the only reason I sought out a psychologist. I was so ill and traumatized that I couldn't even recognize that I needed help. And the psychologist I found would diagnose me within one meeting with PTSD and acknowledge the real trauma at the heart of my dysfunction, the death of my child, and the second trauma that broke it open wide, the betrayal from my partner.

"Your grandma June says, 'I love you Erin and I want nothing but happiness for you. You need to find it and let go of what has been holding you down and making you ill. There will be life after loving such a precious child. Enjoy the ones you have with you. Ava is in good hands. Stay focused on healing yourself. And she is saying her legs don't hurt anymore?'"

Yes. My grandmother June was the epitome of class, well known, and a straight shooter. I miss her terribly and love her wholly. I still have her very first voting card for women. A memento and truth of the things she was most proud of through the eras and changes in her life. My grandfather died when I was a baby and she would refuse to start a relationship with anyone else for the rest of her life. She had severe arthritis in her hands, her hips, her knees, her ankles, and her feet. Her legs hurt constantly and no pharmaceutical concoction touched the pain she endured for the last ten years of her life. Jade could never have known this and acknowledged that it didn't make sense to her, questioning it as she wrote it.

"She is also saying that your partner is not the man for you and not the one who will help you through this all. Stay strong and stay positive. The truth has now set you free. They're saying he is not good for you. You need to work on yourself and own well-being. Your grandma is saying you don't need him. You are strong and will do much better on your own."

I replied to this with my heart opened so wide that I couldn't contain my joy, the love that filled my body. "Grandma, this is the truth. I miss you."

My grandmother's spirit was right on cue with Jade, acknowledging the truth of my now ex-partner. The truth of me and where I was at, knowing all that had come to pass left me shattered. "I miss you too honey but I am right here with you all the time."

Two days before Jade and I had this surprise conversation, I was sitting in my bedroom calling, in thought, to Grandma June and Ava for direction, for help. And suddenly in that moment, I felt someone breathing on my cheek. I held my breath to be sure that's what I felt. Definitely, someone was very close to me softly breathing at my cheek. I knew it was my Grandmother immediately, inexplicably without a doubt. I had not told Jade that I had asked for help, and blurted out my truth to my Grandmother and to her, *I felt you on Sunday Grandma, did you hear me calling you and Ava?*

"I feel so light and happy right now Erin," said Jade, "I'm pretty sure I'm being shown how you're feeling. Like a thousand bricks have been lifted. Grandma June says she came to you to give me a sign to get my butt in gear and give you the messages. She says your partner is a stick in the mud and that is where he deserves to stay. Move on. Kick him to the curb. You have had too many men treat you like garbage. Don't let them do this to you anymore. Girl power, she says." It was like Jade was my Grandmother, speaking just like my grandmother, her tone, her phrasing, her strength. Jade commented on my Grandmother now too, "Oh, your grandma makes me laugh, she doesn't hold back." Indeed, this was my beloved Grandmother June.

There have been an odd amount of red cardinals and an abundance of delicate white butterflies all around me in the last few years. They flutter directly in front of me, swooping and swirling, dancing with joy. I've noticed their perfectly balanced bodies and magical wings created by God. I would watch with childlike wonder at the beauty in their dance.

I couldn't place the significance or why it felt special to me that they would cross my path so frequently, until Jade continued with her message questioningly, "Erin do you ever see red cardinals around you? And butterflies? This is your baby girl. She is around you all the time. Ava is asking me to talk to you in person about her, to meet with you. But she is also asking me to tell you these other things too. Ava says she wants you to know how she came through to me for the first time."

Jade was so open about the newness and how these strange things occurred for her, just as Ava asked her to.

"I was lying in bed with my daughter and I heard the Bette Midler song, 'Wind Beneath My Wings.' I asked who was there and heard 'Ava' as clear as day. She then asked me if I could give her mommy a message. She said, 'I am the same age as her.' My heart melted. Ava is six when she comes through and her voice sounds just like a six-year-old." On the day that Jade and I had this conversation, my daughter Ava would have been six years old and one month away from her seventh birthday. The significance of this was not lost on me. I realized that this was a year of sevens. Ava died in the seventh month of the year. It was Ava's seventh birthday and the seventh anniversary of her death. My phone number, which I got exactly seven years before, has three sevens in it. It was also the year 2017 at that moment, and I was turning thirty-seven in this same year. The number seven was making its presence and pattern known. The things that we dub as coincidences, would start happening all the time for me. But only as long as I was not lost in my head, in thoughts. I had to be in the present moment to catch all the signs I was being sent. I had to start listening instead of thinking all the time. I've learned that there is no such thing as a coincidence, but in truth, are actually divinely timed signs for you and signals guiding you, confirming you, warning you, lifting you up. They are letting you know that you are safe, held in the hands of the universe and loved beyond measure and to trust the rollercoaster we call life.

Jade never asked me for anything, no payment, no reciprocation of any kind. She said that my healing and happiness was the gift. My daughter Ava would then orchestrate, through Jade, a one-day retreat for me to be a part of called a heal and release. Jade went out and bought this retreat and enrolled me in it, with a letter from Ava and a bracelet that said PEACE on it. She gave without expectation for a return, "Ava asked me to do this, she said you needed this. It is a gift. I don't want you to pay for this, it is a gift from Ava and I am just grateful and blessed to be able to give you her messages." Jade embodies humility and kindness and has a softness to her that is comforting to me, a kinship of sorts is felt throughout me, like she is one of the sparkling strands in the web that connects and crosses in different places of my life and my heart. My daughter would ask Jade to write me a love letter from her, word for word, to give to me. My love letter was exquisitely painful, infused with pure love:

I love you so much it hurts. I understand how you think and feel about me every day. You must know, Mommy, that my passing was truly the divine plan, as hard as it was on you and Daddy. Mommy, you need to learn and figure out how to do this. You can still love me, miss me, but also move on. Your health problems are a manifestation of your loss, losing me. The pain and grief you feel inside is eating away at you and it hurts me to watch this from above. It is not your time to be here with me but you need to choose to live, to be with Domenic and Gabriella and live a happy healthy life knowing that I am with you every day. Loving you, playing with you all, and still very much a part of this family. Celebrate me. Don't mourn me, for I am just a thought away and right beside you. I am red cardinals and white butterflies.

My lungs and heart work great up here. This is where I was meant to grow up and be your baby from above, your daughter in heaven. Don't get and stay angry, for anger will only hurt you more and you can't take anymore. Your health is very critical and you need to choose to live, live for your earth babies. Please go see a psychologist, you need to release your anger and fully grieve my loss. Mommy you will be so surprised how much better you will feel. You'll feel amazing and have more energy. It will help fix your broken heart. When you listen to the song "I Believe I Can Fly" you can smile in knowing I am there, soaring above you, smiling right back at you, instead of crying over losing me. You haven't lost me, my body is gone but my soul is still very much alive and living.

I promise I will help you and be there with you along the whole way. Way to recover from a broken heart. Isn't that funny, now I am helping you with your broken heart. Laugh, Mommy, it is funny. I love you Mommy and I can't wait to help fix your broken heart. Live, Laugh, and Love again.

Love Ava

My heartache would take on a life of its own as I read this love letter. Tears of joy and pain streamed down my face. The ache would swell larger, gaping with emotion, at the start of every sentence and then as I felt my daughter's truth, my truth, at the end of each sentence, the gaping hole would become slightly smaller, contracting with a soothing ripple of love.

My daughter's death destroyed me and yet her spirit would lift me from the burdens of my pain and sorrow. Here she was, seven years later, picking me up and loving every hurt I had, cherishing me in all my brokenness, giving me a hand to lead the way out of the darkness of despair. Miraculously, proving to me that death is not the end, that my child is not dead in the context that we, as humans perceive it as.

I felt exhilarated and humbled at the broken concepts of this world, that made it so hard to live without my daughter. Ava was telling me what I needed to know. The truth.

That unequivocally and irrevocably she is alive and everywhere. Our souls are infinite like the flapping of the hummingbird wings, forever unbroken, a constant. The spirit of death is life. Our body isn't 'life' at all. Our souls and energy are life. We simply change our energy to a physical form to experience, to connect, to love and to learn.

We've just got this whole concept of death completely wrong! Our bodies are technically just energy, our souls are also energy and energy doesn't just die and disappear never to be again. It simply changes, disperses into different forms and then forms other shapes. It flows with ease through all its changes, knowing that it is unending. This was a turning point in how I perceived myself and the foundation of beliefs that we all build our lives upon in this society when it comes to death.

This love letter would teach me that I can do this. I falsely believed that I needed permission to live again and to love again. I couldn't see that it was okay to just be me in the present, knowing that she is forever and I am forever. That's just not what I was taught, nowhere close to what we are groomed to believe about this life. Why didn't they teach us that we are all forever infinitely loved and an array of energy, all from the same place? What if the past life concepts and beliefs are actually other molecules of energy from before that have formed with our energy in this life, and this is why we hold memories from 'other lives,' each of us born with our own distinct personality with a melding of energy from other lives.

Ava's ashes, the last physical form of my love, lived in a dark closet in my home for seven years. Just like my grief and inability to accept her loss that was also in the darkest closet of my soul. After separating, in a fleeting moment of peace between us, Evan and I found the perfect garden, the perfect place to honour Ava, to let her rest, to give peace to all that walked through these gardens. A beautifully detailed stone bench with a high back and vines intertwining all around the bench were etched into an intricate trellis pattern that covered it. The day we found this bench, Ava showed us that she was with us, looking up at the sky, a giant 'A' was clearly marked by the planes – undeniable and awe inspiring that we are not alone, that she felt the joy I was feeling. The bench would be set permanently into the earth and surrounded by the most exquisite perennial gardens. We planted a white lilac with a stone placed below it, engraved with a devotion of love to her and the dates of her life and death. This would all culminate and be completed on her seventh birthday. Words can't explain the feeling, the knowing, that I was being held in the palms of the universe, completely connected and loved with Ava right beside me. This was where she wanted to be laid to rest. This place would be the anchor for me to set her free, to set myself free. I felt like I was soaring, such joy and elation in knowing that this was truly her place for her and I to be at peace. And this garden was filled with white butterflies. Dozens of them dancing with delight around me, sitting on her bench, dusting the flowers with magic and love. It is so important that you make a place to honour your child that you can go to. It doesn't need to be a cemetery or an altar. I find that a garden allows you to meander, to ponder in delight at the first new sprouts each year, a reminder that life is infinite and that death is impermanent. This should be a place that you can cry tears of sorrow one day and smile through them the next day. It will be the place your souls will intertwine and just be.

Five weeks later, on the seventh anniversary of her death, my mother and I, along with my children, would go to Ava's garden and sprinkle her ashes around the white lilac, gently folding them back into the earth with love. Ashes to ashes, dust to dust. My delight in knowing that this was exactly what Ava wanted pulled me to send a message to Jade. I told her where she could find Ava's garden. And she would go there, to sit with my daughter. *I went to Ava's memorial spot at lunch today. There were several white butterflies around while I sat there, very peaceful. I feel I connected with Ava and as we talked it sounded like a poem. So I started writing as I heard it; This is where I lay, this is where I'll be when my Mom comes to visit me. Through good days and bad days she's got an escape, where I lay and wait for a well reunited visit. I am with her always in heart but here is where she will feel our connection, our souls together as one. I am here for all to see, to come and visit with me. My true soul never rests, but finds peace in the memorial for me. May she rest, with peace knowing I am here in ashes but my soul lives on inside of all of us. Rest in peace knowing I am free like a butterfly.* Jade ended this confirming and validating that Ava knew exactly how I felt, *Ava says to me about you; Her heart is healing back together again. She's released me, released the burden of my death. I am now pure joy in her heart and loved ones and you. Till we meet again, Ava.*

Both Jade and I sat in the sheer power and love of my daughter's all-knowing wisdom and joy. The truth of it all. That we were witness to it.

On this same day, the anniversary of Ava's death, Evan was in Japan on a self-dubbed journey of self-realization. I hoped he would find forgiveness for himself and all that had shaped his perspective of life and actions. He wanted me to spread Ava's ashes on her death anniversary to culminate with his reaching the top of Mount Fuji. I agreed, thinking how freeing it would be for him. My innocent thought of joy for him at this idea would be so far from the truth. In the middle of that night on the anniversary of her death, I received a message from him. A suicide letter with love, shame, and forgiveness. It ended with his prayer and wishes to join his daughter now.

This was what I got up to in the morning following the ceremony of love that I'd given for Ava. I felt panicked, doubting if it was real, fearful and feeling responsible because I'd ended the relationship. Feeling that I had the power to change this outcome. In my head, I went over all of the conversations, events, and letters leading up to this moment. Were there other signs to confirm this was real? Does he fit the classic indicators of suicidal? He's in another country on top of Mt Fuji. How could anyone reach him? I started to send him messages. "Call me, we need to talk about this, you have an amazing life ahead of you." No response. I waited a few hours before I met with my psychologist and showed her the message.

"Has he given away any of his belongings?" she asked. Looking back, yes, he had. He had said he had left boxes of his things at random people's houses that he had stayed at just before he left for Japan. I told him he should get them and I would store them for him in the basement till he was back. "It doesn't matter, I don't need that stuff anyways," he had said to me.

The psychologist continued with her questions, "Has he mentioned anything about saying goodbyes to people or anything like that?"

My heart stopped at this and fear settled in, "Yes, he did." I remembered him sitting beside me on the back stairs, a sense of peace with the sun shining down on us a few days before he was scheduled to fly out. *I have a few people to see that have given meaning in my life. People who will no longer be a part of my life. Some of them, I just need to say my piece to before I go. Maybe I'll write them letters – no, I need to see them in person.* A feeling of happiness came over me after he said that. I had thought we could go our separate ways and still love each other as human beings, all forgiven, the journey honoured, and we would both be okay. That we were both going to have true happiness. The recognition of what he was actually saying hit me full force in my psychologist's office.

He had been preparing. He had been giving cryptic messages that I just wasn't following. I'm a "what you see is what you get" kind of girl, no cryptic message needed, no hidden agenda beneath the exterior. He was always cryptic, always had a hidden agenda. How had I not connected these dots? How could I live with myself if I didn't help him?

My psychologist cut to the chase after a few more questions confirmed, "Erin, you need to call one of his family members. You, or they, need to contact the embassy there. There is an emergency number for Mount Fuji in Japan. I'll find it for you right now. Don't panic. He is in another country and you cannot control someone else's actions and choices.

His letter is highly indicative of committing suicide. Couple that with the facts you've just confirmed, which are all of the standard actions of someone intending to end their life.

Call a member of his family who is still speaking with you. Tell them that I am advising you in my professional opinion, given all of this information, that he is high risk – he's still grieving the death of his child, the death of his mother, the loss of his relationship with his spouse, his whole life has fallen out from under him, too. And there are classic signs of mania in a lot of the interactions you've described while he has been travelling and corresponding with you. Maybe all this is coincidence and he isn't going to commit suicide – "

I interrupted her, words frantically scrambling out of my mouth – "What if it isn't? What if I can stop this? I can't live with myself if that is what is to come and I just sat by hoping it was coincidence."

"Exactly, Erin. Make the call. Do what you can."

Japan was Evan's second trip in three months, each trip spanning almost a month. He left in May and was only home for a few weeks around Ava's birthday in June and then left in July again for Japan. Prior to Japan, he had gone to Italy, to experience his roots and his mom's side of the family. He then flew from Italy over to the Netherlands for a while to experience his roots on his father's side. I corresponded with him the entire time on these trips and I supported that he had wanted to take them for years. I agreed I would look after the kids while he went travelling around the world, trying to find himself. He would include me in his extreme highs and lows on these trips. Some of them I feel were divine intervention from Ava for him – she was watching over him, loving him, holding his hand. And other things that happened were the side effects of a life filled with blame, fear, and guilt, that clouded his lens of the world around him.

Truth be told, I panicked on the inside. Running to my car the moment I stepped outside the psychologist's office. I sped all the way home, calling Evan's cousin the moment I got in the door.

I left a message, hung up the phone, and kept repeating out loud, "Please call me back, please call me back, please call me back."

And his cousin did. Evan and his cousin were like siblings. They lived across the street from each other, they were the same age, their mothers were sisters and tightly knit together. They all loved Evan like a son, whatever he needed, they would give the shirt off their back, they were family. I loved this about them. They were warm and welcomed me into their lives with open arms. His cousin's voice was panicked on the phone, "Erin, what's happened? Is he okay?" I would tell him that I received a message in the middle of that night that seemed like a suicide note. I told him how I let the psychologist read it to see if maybe I was assuming things or overreacting.

"You do know that he tried to commit suicide when we were teenagers, right?"

What? No, I didn't know this. "He didn't tell you this?" he asked incredulously.

"No, he didn't," I replied in shock. Just like all of the other secrets and lies I had been told and not told over the last ten years. I'd had no idea. It would dawn on me in my mind's eye in that moment that I had a clear conversation with him and in my ignorance and naivety had said that I didn't understand how someone could kill themselves – I had said that to someone whom I loved, who had tried to kill himself, who had been in so much pain that he felt death was the only way out. And I had no idea, completely oblivious. This is why Evan had never told me about it. "I will send you the message he sent and you tell me what you get from this," I said.

After sending it, his cousin confirmed that it definitely seemed to be a suicide note. He called him, also frantic to get a response, at the thought of the person we all loved ending it.

My calling his cousin enraged Evan enough to respond to everything after that. He would act normal with his cousin, making jokes with him, and in the next message, berate me for being what he called a selfish and disgusting human being. It would mark the beginning of a year and half of him battering me, blaming me for ruining his life, for being responsible for Ava's death. He felt I was turning his family against him, for destroying our own family by separating. This was the outcome of trying to help him, of making one phone call to make sure he knew he was loved, to make sure he lived so he could have a happy life at the end of it and watch his son grow up. Maybe I didn't make the right decision to call his cousin. It was one of those moments in life where you know the choice you make can save a life or end it. I would make the choice to save it and I don't regret making that call, despite the backlash for it. I genuinely love him as a human being, as the father of my children, in all his misery and blame.

Just a few days after this, Jade sent me a message, "Erin, I keep hearing to ask you how Evan is? I had a date with Ava at her bench. I would say, 'I am coming, Ava' and she would keep saying, 'I am here.' I knew I had to talk with her, I knew it couldn't wait." Jade knew a part of what had gone on, the basis of it. Confirming the truth of what had just occurred days before. We both were at a loss for words, both shocked, both hoping that this was a turning point for Evan to get back on track and live his life. But that hope was fleeting.

Over the next twelve months, Jade would reach out to me at the request of Ava sometimes and other times my Grandmother. The two of them would let Jade know when things weren't good for me. They also made aware when I wasn't safe and to tell me. She would touch base with me randomly through the months, sometimes after four months of not talking. Jade would pop into my life with exact timing that could only have been orchestrated by Spirit. "Erin I'm hearing safety first for you. They're saying put another deadbolt on your door. Don't let him into your home. There are hidden intentions. You are protected, do not be scared. They're saying he isn't okay right now. Call the police if anything is amiss, anything strange." And I would wake two days later in the dark of the night to someone outside my home. The darkness hiding the face that was crouched down against the garage, trying to rig the underside of my car for something. My daughter and grandmother would shield me and guide me. All I had to do was trust in the them, in Spirit, in the universe.

What Spirit Wants

We are held in the infinite and loving hands of the universe. We are all imperfect and weighted by the burdens that this world's beliefs hold us to. The weary and downtrodden, the victims and the perpetrators. Death is not the end – in fact, our souls are the life, not the body. And our souls connect and pass by each other, some to touch us, some to break us, some to lead us or simply give a helping hand. We are all energy colliding with each other at times through anger and then lovingly melting into each other at other times. The ebb and flow, the up and down. All movement of energy changing form. There is no death. Spirit has confirmed that this is just an experience, we choose how we live, what we tolerate, which path we will walk down at every step of the way. You can always make a different choice. You can always ask for help. You can have peace, knowing that your child is alive and well, cheering for you every step of the way. They are moving and changing energy to connect with you in all ways, be it hummingbirds, or butterflies, or billboard signs, or people that cross your path. They are there, smiling down at you, just like Ava said in her love letter. Live, Laugh, and Love again.

Your child sees everything from Spirit. Feels all of your emotions, experiences every one of your thoughts. Spirit wants to hold you and guide you to heal your heart so that you can move forward and live again, while loving them. I am living proof that the grass is greener on the other side of your heartache. Let Spirit heal your broken heart, feel them all around you. There is nothing they won't do to make themselves known to you, to help you. All you need to do is stop, clear your mind, live in the moment and trust all that comes to you through signs. If you feel good, you are in the flow of it, able to recognize them as they're presented. If you have a bad feeling, trust your instinct, your soul, and keep yourself away from that situation.

If I can do this and know this truth deep within myself and come to a place of peace and joy in knowing that my child's spirit is always around me, you can do this too. If you are reading this book, it's highly likely that Spirit has orchestrated it coming into your hands. They want you to see them in a different light – it is the light of truth. The invisible divine guidance coaxing you to see them, to feel them, to trust them, to help you heal your heart. You've got nothing to lose and everything to gain. Spirit wants only the best for you in your healing and will always provide you with what you need, which path to take, to trust your intuition. And here you are.

Miracles will unfold, but only if you allow them to.

The Signs of Spirit

"Love is the bridge between you and Everything."
– Rumi

The signs of Spirit are everywhere, coincidences at every turn if you are open to it. Trusting is the hardest thing to do, in a world that scoffs at the unseen and teaches you to fear and go for safety and security at all costs. I have always had an interest in the unseen, the art of herbal magic, tinkering with Wicca and crystals, angels and ghosts, all as a teenager. A phase, maybe, but I've never outgrown the piqued interest in all things Spirit, the magic of it all. It had always been in my heart, deep in the cracks and crevices, despite everyone's dismissal of it.

Along the story of my last eight years, I've left out some fascinating signs that Spirit sent me along the way, as well as premonitions that I refused to accept, but my soul felt the truth of them no matter how many lies I told myself. After Ava came home from the children's hospital at ten days old, I was meticulous with her injections, the way I washed her, the angle I held her. I was overbearing with others who would help or hold her. The fear that something could be done the 'wrong' way and result in Ava going back to the hospital was palpable when someone was in the room with me. When Ava was three and a half weeks old, I was following the routine that I had set with her, totally focused on changing her dressing and packing the hole in the side of her chest. Suddenly, I had a vision, a premonition. I was in another place and could see my shoes and the woman's shoes beside me. I was talking to her clear as day, "I know what it's like to lose a child, too." Then she started speaking and it was muffled, I couldn't make out her words. But my words were clear and concise, no mistaking them nor the sadness and tone in them and I felt like I was that woman in her bones. Not the woman standing over her baby and changing her dressings. And then, just like that, it was gone. And I was right where I was a second before, changing Ava's dressing, the same woman that was changing her dressing. Why on earth would I be saying that? I'm losing my mind – what a horrible thought. My denial of the feeling of it and the words I said just weren't real. I would make lots of excuses for this occurrence, right up until I gave up. But the truth is, I knew deep in my soul that it was real, no matter how much I tried to change it in my thoughts. Let's not forget about the two women who also told my mother that my daughter would be bringing me a boy. And the connection of it all was in Ava's love letter to me, "You must know, Mommy, that my passing was truly the divine plan." I do know this, the truth rings clearly in it now.

Just a few months before Ava was born, a divinely orchestrated string of events would set in motion the discovery of her heart defects. At the time, I had no idea that it would lead to Ava living for five weeks versus the one day it would have been had all of it not taken place. I was watching my oldest niece and nephew in addition to Gabriella. I have always believed that my niece was connected and felt a lot of different energies around her. She got angry with me, for no reason – it was sudden. And she decided to run away. I knew I couldn't run after her, seven months pregnant and waddling. So I grabbed her arms, trying to redirect her back up the driveway into the house. She whipped around and lashed out with her leg, which hit me in the stomach. I doubled over. And she was gone down the street. Gabriella would start crying as she and I started chasing after my niece. Once we finally got home with her forty-five minutes later, I had an ache in my abdomen. I knew that my niece had no idea what all had happened and what it could mean, but I also knew that my baby was fine but for some reason I wanted an ultrasound, just to be safe, just a weird feeling. My sister-in-law felt terrible I'm sure at all of this, bless her heart. But that visit to the doctor would lead to multiple ultrasounds and the discovery that Ava had multiple heart defects, and that one would close within hours of her being born, shutting down the blood flow and her heart. She needed heart surgery after being born. Looking at this now, my niece got upset as part of the divine purpose to give my daughter a longer life – more time for me to love her. I got five and a half weeks instead of five hours with Ava. This is all thanks to my niece, who was true to her spirit and emotion that day. She gave me a gift and no one could see the gift. I am forever grateful to my niece for this. Everything happens for a reason, even if that reason doesn't come to light until months, years, or even decades later.

I've learned that songs are a valuable and deeply connected tool for Spirit to connect with us. A song has the power to lift you and move you, to caress the emotion that you are feeling, be it good or bad. Music is truly at the heart and soul of us all. It is something that we all relate to and can connect with that reverberates in our souls. Ava and Grandma June come to me with songs. I never know who is sending it or when I'll get one, but when I do it is striking, there is no mistaking it is from Spirit and I'm left enveloped in deep gratitude and feeling of belonging in and to the universe. I would wake up with a start in the mornings and a song would be playing in my head unmistakably clear and with purpose. The lyrics would always be relevant to something I had been asking about or my request to be given a sign. Ask and you shall receive. The radio is also an often-used tool. I often get into my car and tune into a select few radio stations. I like the Magic station and the Faith station – apparently Spirit likes those too, go figure! I would ask to be played a song that will give me a sign, or hope, or help. Spirit almost always delivered on this. I would ask and the next song to play would be 'I Believe I Can Fly.' Or I would worry about a situation and ask to be given some guidance and the next song would be George Michael, 'You gotta have faith, faith, faith.' They would be songs that were unmistakably relevant to the questions I was asking or the emotion I was feeling. There was no denying that Spirit orchestrated it. Divine timing.

I'll never forget the day that I was sitting on Ava's bench, eyes closed and connecting with her. Suddenly, I heard the lyrics to a Justin Bieber song, "When it comes to you, there's no crime. Let's take both of our souls and intertwine." These lyrics kept replaying as I sat in the stillness of the garden. My heart was confused at these lyrics. I opened my eyes to see my ex standing in front of me. I was scared to rock the boat, scared to stand up for myself after the turmoil he was causing over the last few months. I tried to get him to see what he was doing. I tried to be understanding. The conversation led to him sitting down beside me on Ava's bench, looked me straight in the eye, "It's your fault our daughter is dead, you smoked while you were pregnant with her. I blame you." Fear would coat my throat and paralyze my limbs for moments on that bench. But I would get up and go to my car and hightail it out of there as fast as I could. I know firsthand the pure rage that fuels the blame when your child is dead. I now have an understanding that we all have the capacity to hurt others in certain situations, especially that involve your children dying, or suffering or being abused. On her very own bench, the sacred place where I savoured her memory and rejoiced in her soul – this is where I was blamed by her father for her death. Spirit was sending me that song, with those lyrics, to prepare me and comfort me for what was about to take place with him.

The power of song and lyrics is amazing. When I think of all the artists who truly bare their souls in their writing and their music, those are the ones that are helping the masses. Those are the songs that we find comfort in, guidance in and a feeling of belonging, that we are not alone. Kesha is one of those artists, moving her trauma to her music. Her song 'Praying' was like a movement for me. A helping leg up to forgiveness of my ex. It's like I've had a year and a half of events that require forgiveness and empathy for him. Every onslaught of attacks every seven to fourteen days now, required me to internally assess and forgive him. I'm no longer a victim, and his words are not my truth. They are his truth. I have empathy for him and forgiveness, for he knows not what he is truly doing and who knows, maybe I needed one hundred lessons in forgiveness over and over and over, one after the other. And I take comfort in laying down the burden and dysfunction of co-dependency and giving that to Spirit, to God.

I often think of my mother-in-law, Theresa, a deeply faithful Catholic woman. Just a few weeks ago, I focused my energy and asked her to give me a sign that my ex and my son and daughter would be okay, asking her to help them. A few days later, a rosary with Mother Theresa would arrive at my mother's house in the mailbox. Out of nowhere, not affiliated with anything my family would do, think, say or attend. My mom knew right away handing it to me, "This isn't for me, it's likely for you from Theresa." My mother had no idea I'd asked Theresa for a sign. But here it was. A comfort, a confirmation. These are things that are brushed away as coincidence. They are not. Just like the tingling you get when something is off. In hindsight, your tingling was always proven to be spot on, without reason. Jade too, had confirmed before for me when I was worried about my ex and his wellbeing, "Your grandma says just know this will all be over soon my dear. Hang in there and don't let him into your house. Rest assured you will all be fine but don't take any chances, lock and deadbolt your doors. Your grandma wants for you to know not to carry his burdens, they are not yours. He has his people and angels too. To tell you that you are not responsible for his actions." All confirmations of my thoughts and questions in my head that Spirit hears all the time. "I'm hearing you will have more to face, just under a year from now. October. Not sure what that means. Ava is here now, saying she will look after Daddy? Do you know what that means?" Jade asked.

I had asked Ava in my thoughts to look out for Evan and help him to heal. Jade also indicated early on when speaking with my grandmother and Ava that Ava loves her father and doesn't speak ill of him. All things related to my ex were discussed by my grandmother to me. I have an understanding deep in my soul that he too is struggling in the underbelly of grief and the emotions and thoughts that take hold of you. I realize now that I cannot help someone who doesn't want to be helped, who treats me like a punching bag when I do try and help.

Jade also talked about my sister's daughter, Sophia, and the connections are astounding. Sophia and Ava were born three weeks apart. Sophia never met Ava in the flesh, and wouldn't remember it if she did anyways, or so we thought. At four and five years old, Sophia would make me cards from Ava, with pictures of all of us outlined saying "I love you" and would sign them 'Love Ava.' I never understood why she did this, but it brought me to tears and put the defrost on my heart, if only for that moment in time. My sister told me a few years later that Sophia would get upset at night and sob, saying, "I miss Ava, I miss Ava." My sister and her partner had thought Sophia was just using that as an excuse for why she was behaving that way – she never knew Ava, and we still weren't talking about Ava at all, so after months of this they finally told Sophia they didn't want her to say it again. Jade asked me at one point, "Does Sophia talk about dreams or connecting with a little girl Ava?" Then I told Jade what my sister had described. "This makes sense. They are very connected together, she is actually missing Ava and is losing the connection as she gets older and knows it. Ava and Sophia are like soul sisters." Jade's words were piecing the puzzle together like a map, as she said them. That explained her writing me cards from Ava, her crying every night saying she missed her. It also explained why, when Sophia and I would be together out of earshot of others, she would take my hand and say, "It's okay, Auntie E." In her younger years she always wanted to be with her Auntie E, despite how un-fun I was most of the time, bless her heart. Sophia has always held a special place in my heart. She touches my soul often. I love her like she is my own daughter and I feel a deep connection with her as I do my own children.

Jade explained that children are deeply connected, and it pulled on her heart strings. I've witnessed and heard things from both my nieces, my nephews, and my children that would cement this belief. They are so close to Spirit, to themselves. When Domenic was four years old, he was afraid of the water, a giant fear that both he and Gabriella unexplainably shared right from birth. And one day out of the blue he said, "Mommy, you need to get your boat license. We have to get one to drive the boat." I brushed this off because I had no idea what he was talking about – he didn't even like water. And this would continue, for two weeks straight. He was adamant that I had to get this boat license. Another week later, my uncle would ask my sister and

I if we wanted to buy his sailboat. It was like a light bulb went off. My son was being guided to guide me to the next step on my journey. Despite everyone telling me it was a bad idea, that I couldn't do it on my own, that it wasn't safe for the kids - I did it. I bought it. Fear would stop me from learning it for the first summer. By the time the next summer came around, I would be in a much better place to face my fear. I showed up, my children and I made memories like we've never been able to make before. We took risks that allowed us to see that we could have fear, face it, do it, and come out the other side stronger.

My children are the light of my life, and I have learned to let go of the idea that they are a reflection of me, that I need to control them. They have their own lessons, their own journey and life experience that I cannot control. They've guided me, helped me, and loved me in all my brokenness. In all my thoughts of how parenting should be, they forgive and love me anyways. They have been my greatest teachers at times. And then I think how lucky I am to have two children teaching me here right beside me and I also have Ava teaching me from above. I'm surrounded in an abundance of love. My perspective used to be that I was surrounded with loss, but Ava has taught me that it is the opposite. It's a simple matter of perspective, of the lens you choose to colour your view with. Spirit only wants the truth to come to light, to show the way, to heal our misguided beliefs about who we are and what our purpose is.

The joy and peace you will feel in this is priceless, immeasurable, pure joy to your soul. Sandra, another bereaved parent, also discovered this joy and recounts how this knowing gave her strength to keep walking forward, to live again, to love and grow. "My son passed away suddenly and unexpectedly. I found him lying on the floor. There was nothing I could do. The shock of it all, to find your child lifeless. He was my world, my only son, we did everything together. It was so hard and people really don't understand unless they've been there. But I know my son is with me, he is sending me signs everywhere. All the things he loves and the things we did, he is showing me that he is here all the time. I know without a doubt that his spirit is connected to me in life and death. I talk to him all the time. If I didn't know this I would not have been able to go on. And if I were to tell people these things, they'd think I was crazy – there are a lot of non-believers, but I don't care. This is my truth."

It never ceases to amaze me that every bereaved parent I have had the pleasure of speaking with and working with that has this knowledge of Spirit, this knowing that their child is not gone – Are also the ones who have found joy in the sorrow. They are the ones who are able to walk through their grief, that have real hope that grows. They are the ones with peace in their hearts, who can move forward in life while honouring their child, because they are taking their child with them as they move forward. They grow and discover the power of Spirit and their true authentic selves. You can do this, too. You can experience all of it – the only thing you need to do is be open to it.

I had to learn how to see the signs once Jade had come to me, once I knew without a doubt that my daughter was there and I could talk to her anytime I wanted and that she was listening. At times it was difficult because I was so involved in the circumstances and events of each day. But when I was able to quiet my mind and focus on my heart and my soul and with intention, this was where the miracles showed themselves. And I would learn that these miracles were everywhere, happening all the time, but we're so busy, so lost in thought, that we miss them.

Here are the keys to learning how to open your mind and to see the signs that your child is sending you. The first thing is to ask for a sign, and be specific. The more specific you are, the easier it is for your child to show you their presence in Spirit and the easier it is for you to catch and acknowledge the sign. Ask for something simple, something that has great meaning to you, a song, a symbol, an animal, anything. Second step, and for me, this was the most important – believe. Believe that you will receive this sign you've asked for. Believe that your child is there, no matter how silly you feel or think it may be. The third step is to set that intention of belief while picturing the sign you've asked for in your mind – and then let it go. Let it go so that Spirit can make this happen for you. They want to show you they are there, they want you to see the signs, but you've got to let go of the control.

Once you start to do these steps and learn to be in the moment, it becomes easier and easier. More and more synchronicities and signs will reveal themselves to you. Your child wants you to connect with them – so let's do this!

Chapter 9

Death and God

"Seek the wisdom that will untie your knot.
Seek the path that demands your whole being."

– RUMI

As a society we've assigned the word Death as a finite term, understood by many as 'the end.' We don't discuss death and grief, rarely give it the space it requires, despite it being the most universal experience for all humans, all animals, all creatures. It's an uncomfortable topic, the intensity of emotions is great discomfort for most. Death is a subject that no one has a definitive scientific explanation for. Our greatest minds of this century have discovered, researched, and explored the process of illness and death on the body, but what about the soul? What about God? What about Spirit? What about all the miracles that are totally unexplainable in a scientific context?

Beliefs shape and mold our thought process every day. It is fascinating that God is so tightly reined to religions. When I talk about God, I don't associate the word with any religion. My truth is that God is part of me and I am part of God, unending. I believe we all are One. We're taught of a God who wields a sword of judgement and punishment. We're taught to fear or we shall be stricken down, those that do not believe in him. We are teaching that fear, a.k.a. God, is the maker and taker of life. Fear, a.k.a. God, is the decider of how your life will be and what will happen. This leads to three very finite beliefs that staunch our creativity and sense of wonder; Fear instead of love. Punish instead of forgive. Victim instead of empowerment. These three beliefs actually force us to compare others to ourselves and ultimately create a wasteland in our wake. How can anything grow and live in Fear? It can't. Nothing can grow and the life of fear is blanketed with thick misery, blame, and shame. How could we ever grieve the death of our loved ones, when we have to consider, or rather worry about, what they did wrong in life, who did they hurt, were they baptized, did they repent? Did they pray enough? No wonder our ability to honour and grieve the tragic loss of a child is so distorted and disconnected. God is simply a belief. That's it. It isn't the truth or a lie, neither right nor wrong. You can literally have a belief about anything, anyone, and that belief becomes your truth.

Our beliefs prior to the death of a loved one often include the concepts of heaven and hell through society and western Christianity. The framework for these taught beliefs surrounding religion and God are heavily woven into the fabric of our lives, from the first year you come into this world.

Atheists are shunned for believing in nothing – is there really a true atheist that believes in nothing, is nothing their personal truth? How awful grieving must be in that belief system too. The belief taught to us is of a God who is punishing and unforgiving. That you will be judged to get to the land of happiness or the fiery bellows of hell. This creates a society that is rampant with guilt and shame. Discrediting our ancestors and blaming what's come before us for what is now. Every moment of every day we have a choice, choose the same steps, the same path, and you will get the same results, the same belief, and the same outcome. All because of a belief, a tape that replays that same belief, reaction, and outcome, over and over.

I've got a new tape. One that is recorded in truth of Spirit. One that allows me to create and mold and give purpose to every thought, every desire.

One that allows me to love myself in the imperfection of it all. A tape that doesn't replay itself unless I choose it to. This tape connects me to everyone I've ever loved and has loved me, to forgive them, to love them, to be in the divine presence of all. Again, like being held in the palms of the universe and weathering every storm without despair, because I know and trust from every molecule of energy in my body, brain, and soul, that I am exactly where I'm supposed to be, no matter the circumstance, no matter the loss, no matter the heartbreak. It is a hard concept to hear when you are grieving a child. I fought it like I was losing my mind. I fought it so hard that it ate away at me. The refusal to accept what was, what had happened. The refusal to give up the notion that I was responsible for life and death.

Everything we are is shaped by what we're told, how we're scolded, our education systems, our religions. Every experience can change the lens we see from, either out of fear and shame or out of forgiveness and love. Think about what your belief is about Death and Life. When you stop and contemplate exactly what it is, you can then dive down into where it came from. Was it yours? Was it your parents? Was it a teacher, a relative, a priest, a co-worker, a friend? We tend as human beings to have this innate need to belong. Some of us alter our beliefs to belong, despite our intuition telling us this doesn't feel good, doesn't feel right. And there are others who morph into whatever the belief is, so that they can fully belong in a tribe. They say that we often become most like the people we surround ourselves with. And they often hold a similar belief system, or the counter belief system that allows the two beliefs to co-exist, kind of like a codependent relationship. I've been that person, with one belief about myself, because that's what others told me I was. And I would continually put myself in situations and connect with people who would uphold that belief. I did it subconsciously. It was so engrained in the conceptual idea of who I was that I didn't even stop to consider why I thought that was who I was. Beliefs can make or break you. They can wrap you in love, or shred you to pieces. Most believe a belief system that is not their own, just like I did.

My daughter's death seriously defied every belief I had. It shackled me to the floor with the chains of yesterday. If I continued to live with the beliefs I had been taught about God, about life, and about myself, I would never have escaped the misery, trapped in fear and despair, punishing myself like I was taught about the God that punishes his children. My fears are based on beliefs, ones that aren't even true. They were part of that old tape that kept replaying. I had to lose so much just to question everything I was taught and believed. Why is that? Why did I need to learn from pain and loss, rather than from joy and abundance? Because of what I believed life was, God was, who I was. They were part of the beliefs that no longer rang true, no longer served me, and only brought me misery. Everything we believe about death is the starting point of how we grieve, how we walk through the pain, how we feel safe. There is nothing safe about dying, about the afterlife – yet there is nothing safe about living, or being a human being. No one wants to talk about death, or the experience of it. We go to grieving groups and read all this information on the stages of grief and how you might feel. They cover it like they are nice clean steps when in fact they are messy, scattered everywhere and all interconnected in some way. And the truth is most bereaved parents don't make it through many stages, as they call it, mostly because of the expectations and dismissal of grief within our western society. What if we were all raised with the belief that death wasn't the end, and wasn't supposed to leave you with suffering? What if death was meant to be a celebration of life, no matter the circumstance, no matter the length, no matter what is left behind in the aftermath? What if their journey, whether it be the doctor, the midwife, the teacher, the janitor, the rocker, the addict, the poet, the dreamer, or the abuser, was meant to be exactly the way it was, without an ounce of shame at our loved one's life? Without the judgement of society's expectations, of a religious God's expectations.

Grieving groups in general address all kinds of emotions we encounter along the path of grieving and yet don't talk about culture, religion, and backgrounds. They will not talk about God, out of respect for everyone's individual beliefs, and that is truly serving all the people in sorrow. And yet, I can't help but feel in my heart that the thing we don't want to talk about when we help others is what drives our belief about death and what happens and what that means to us. It determines our view on our loss and yet it is the one thing no one wants to talk about. This makes grieving ten times harder and misses the underlying belief system and how to deal with it in the most helpful, empathetic way – it is the never-ending unanswered question, which cannot be measured in the simple human form. It is measured by faith, by the soul, by the sheer knowing that there is something besides what I can see, someone invisible talking to you, acknowledging all the signs that are being sent to you every day – if you'll only stop a moment and be present, be listening, be open to believing. Intuition is our greatest sense, yet it is the most controversial sense because others can't see it, touch it, taste it, or physically feel it. The physical has become a cell that we can't think our way out of. Why is this? It is incredible that the masses will follow only what they are told, only what can be measured. Where is the magic, the purpose, the childlike wonder we all possess, but has been shut down by rules, opinions, religions, and schools? Sometimes even our own family shuts us down, for they too have been heavily entrenched in those same beliefs and know not what they do.

Imagine a mother and father who have just lost their child and in shock, grieving heavily. What if their belief was that they truly had not been left by their child – that every day their child was around them, giving them invisible hugs that are as soft as the warm summer breeze? Now imagine that this belief eased the sorrow, just knowing that this is not the end. Yes, they love that child and will miss holding them till the ends of the earth. But because they know it isn't the end and they know that they are surrounded by their child and are supported through their sadness, they did not stay in the bottom of the grieving well. They didn't get stuck down there believing the despair and guilt over the shoulds and coulds that may or may not have led to their child's death. Instead, they are sitting at the edge of the well, having felt all of the emotions that come to you when grieving a child, but allowing the truth of who they are, who their child is and the truth of life, to comfort them and soothe their souls. Spirit, God, the universe will hold them and stroke their heads and light their hearts and take the burden of Control from them. What if they simply surrendered to this belief? Surrendered to what was, the pain, and just sat in it. Just felt it to the depths of their soul, accepted these feelings, let go of the need to know, let go of feeling like they were in control of someone else's life.

Isn't that a large part of what causes our suffering, believing the lie that we are in control of other people's lives, their actions, their feelings? We are not God in and of itself. We are part of God's energy, God's children, moving and changing with the energy of our souls and our bodies. You can only control how you deal with yourself, what you think in your head, what actions you take. Sure, you'll make mistakes for yourself, and likely for others as well, as I did. But the biggest mistake is truly believing that you have a say in who has died, like you could've changed

it. We all want a guarantee and accountability. Well, guess what
– there are no guarantees for anything in this life. We do that to
make ourselves feel better. Our thoughts run amuck with fear
based on untrue beliefs.

Can you imagine if our beliefs were perfectly aligned with
Spirit? Spirit making it known that it was okay to be sad, scared
or defeated, anxious and all other emotions that we have as
human beings. What if we honoured each emotion and looked
at it through the lens of the universe? Through the lens of energy
moving and changing? Can you imagine if we celebrated our
loved one's life when they died – and I mean really celebrated
them – if everyone got a celebration of life at some point. We
need to talk about them, laugh about them, and have meaning
and purpose, no matter the circumstance, no matter the age,
no matter the hopes and dreams that were left unfinished,
unknown. What if we celebrated their remarkable journey as a
human being at the end of it? Why do we only celebrate the
beginnings as a human race? Congratulations on this brand-new
baby who has a whole life ahead of them. Joy and anticipation of
the dreams *we* have for them. Congratulations on the new job,
on the new house, on getting married. And yet when each of
these things come to an end, those too, are things that make us
uncomfortable and that no one wants to talk about, other than
to say "I'm sorry." I'm sorry your marriage failed, I'm sorry you
lost your house, I'm sorry that you were let go from your job.
Why is loss so uncomfortable for us? It is inevitable, the flow
of all of life. Change is what moves us to higher ground, deeper
meaning, a more expressive life. You fall down, you get back up.
Change can be unbearably hard, I will be the first one to raise

my hand to that one and have probably fought against it with every ounce of my being, blaming God, blaming others, blaming myself, every single time. But you know why it's hard? Because we believe it's a bad thing. We are so upset because it doesn't match the picture we had in our minds of how it was supposed to go or what it should've looked like, or what you expected God to give you or change in you or in the circumstance he's put you in. Great expectations, if you will. They are the root of disappointment and sometimes don't allow you to be in the flow of your life. The tape we're taught and playing in our head has expectations based on yesterday's experience that will only lead to more of that same experience. That is not what God or Spirit is intending for us.

An ending to something is almost standardly viewed as a loss when it comes to our society's concepts of success and failure. We don't want to talk about things that are shameful, or that rock the boat from the norm of life. And death is a rock the boat kind of topic, that begs the question of whether it is the ending of the physical body, or is just the end of a specific form that held our soul? Are we not more than this physical body? And isn't the end actually a beginning in and of itself, both for our loved one and for those of us still here on earth? Yes, we grieve for ourselves, we grieve that we can no longer hold them in the same way, talk to them face to face. We also grieve the things we thought we could have done differently. We often live in yesterday, but what we don't realize is that it stunts the unfolding of today, and unconsciously shapes the future. But what if you knew that every event in your life was unfolding perfectly, despite the horror, the hurt, the devastation, the despair? What if you knew it was designed to lead you to something more amazing, more authentic and fulfilling, than anything you could've dreamt of? What if you knew that your child, your loss, your grief, was all meant to lead you to this incredible awareness that was the most painful, most unbearable thing you could imagine, but resulted in the greatest good for you and all involved? This is possible, when you let Spirit lead you, take the wheel, let Spirit love you. Let yourself be cleansed in the light of Spirit and forgiveness. It is your choice to let it in. You have always had a choice, you just weren't taught that you have a choice.

I am blessed and forever grateful that Jade took a leap of faith to connect with my daughter and grandmother, especially when so many do not agree with the things unseen in our world. The concept and belief in Spirit and the unexplainable is still slightly taboo, not really mainstream, not supported and respected the way it should be. It is real, just as you and I, just as churches portray God. Do we make the religion sector taboo because technically they can't scientifically prove it? No, they don't and that's because they are actually corporations, operating through a lens of politics and money. You might think by my views that I am against religions, I am actually not. The basic concept of them rings true for all people – love and goodness. That should be the focus of them, instead of the corporation, the shame, guilt, and fear that is the underbelly of some of them. That is what allows abuse to happen behind closed doors, because there is a reputation on the line, a bottom line to meet. It is their delivery of the love and goodness that they taint with fear in their message. That is what stops me from reaching out to them, that's what keeps me from going to the church of God. But there are many who live in the love of God through a religion and are able to see what the true meaning is and live it. Some religions allow people to find meaning and purpose and love without judgement. We are all the same when it comes down to it. We all cry, we all bleed, we all love, and we all feel pain. No matter which 'God' or universe or Spirit you are praying to, ultimately it is one God, one universe, one spirit, one giant unending, infinite mass of energy that we are all a part of.

It's okay that 'Your God and Spirit' and 'My God or Spirit' have differences in the story, because at the end of the day if you feel supported and loved and share that with others without fear and judgement of any kind, then we're both doing the same thing just in a slightly different way. Just as we all learn in different ways, pray in different ways, sing in different ways, and live in different ways and follow different paths. It is for the same outcome, love.

I lost the love in me as a child. Who I was, was covered in soot, forgotten in the rubble of death. I was broken apart in the blink of an eye as I held my dying child, and the breaking continued, rippling throughout my life. One conversation with Jade was enough to help me let it all fall away from me. Every person, every belief, every thought. I was finally able to step back and take a look at all of my beliefs that stood behind the blame, the guilt, and the anger, the unbearable pain that soaked my whole being. I was finally able to find people who supported me through my grief, to connect with people who understood my sorrow and people who welcomed my daughter's spirit as I did. Without examining our beliefs, we are tied to a life that is not what we would choose. It causes us to feel we do not have a choice, like there is no other option. Ava gave me permission to feel all that I felt, that I regretted, that I felt responsible for. The understanding that we are all one, never-ending and loved, gave me permission to let my heart beat wholly again, whether I wanted to crawl into bed and cry for myself, or shout and dance around with glee. Both I have done countless times since I rediscovered her in my life.

I have found peace and discovered purpose in my life again knowing that my child lives on all around me. Knowing that I am held in the palms of Spirit, the universe, God, whatever you want to call it, is truth, is light, is comfort, is trust, in all that has come to pass and that will be. You are loved and surrounded, it's up to you whether you choose to see it, to feel it, to trust it. You'll never be forgotten. Your child will never leave you. Death does not part us.

Chapter 10

Walking through Grief

"The Wound is the place where the Light enters you."
– RUMI

Here's the raw naked truth of grieving a child. No one can take away the pain that you are feeling. I wish that I could take it away for you, that I could catch your tears and wipe away the sorrow. I wish that I could wave a magical wand and tell you that I can make it go away. I can't. No one can. When my cousin passed away a year and a half ago suddenly and unexpectedly, more than anything I wanted to wipe the slate clean for my aunt, my uncle and my cousins. I wanted to tell them that it was okay. But it wasn't okay, they were embarking on the ocean of grief and there is no blueprint, no map that can guide them, or lead them where I wanted them to go. I learned the hard way that I can't take away their sorrow and I can't make it hurt it any less. But I did learn the unmatched value of holding their hand, being able to be there in the uncomfortable silence of sorrow that hovers around them and weighs them down.

Each child's story is different, no matter the life, the age, the last days of their life, the story that is theirs alone. Each one is unique and complex, filled with joy and sorrow. They are one and the same and yet at the opposite side of the spectrum. What if I told you they meet and melt together at that other end of the spectrum? I want you to know there is no perfect road in this journey, but there is grace and peace in the surrender to what has transpired. There is a space in your heart and soul that is waiting for you to feel all your emotions, all of them. The rage, the guilt, the shame, the regret, the despair and make sure you honour the laughter, the pleasure, the remembering what each moment felt like, because those are the moments that are realest, the moments that cannot be taken from you by death. Feel every one of them even if they bring you tears. Surround yourself only with those that can sit in the silence with you, without judgement, without telling you what you should be feeling, or how to fix it, or to think of happy things instead of sad things – everyone will have an opinion on this. You are the saver of your soul, the master of your emotions, the decider of how you live your life. The death of your child doesn't just challenge your beliefs, it is the decimation of the person you thought you were. This is not without a purpose, without a reason. It is truth, lying in wait for you to uncover it. It is unending love, that is masked as painful grief. Know that you choose what you want your life to be from this point on. That you are the author of your own story, choose your own adventure – you hold the key to everything. The other side of grief is exquisitely filled with joy and sorrow mingled together, waves of both will wash over you sometimes, you will laugh with joy to find the tears of sorrow follow on its heels. This is the true beauty in all that we are when we surrender to it. They will meld and make you whole. More whole than you ever were before. But only if you allow it.

After Ava died, I was so broken that I didn't even know I needed help. And when I tried to reach out to others, they devalued my grief and my daughter's life unknowingly. I met obstacles that were constructed at the base of the framework that our society is built on. I know that many of you will encounter these beliefs and obstacles through your journey. Do not let them define you, nor destroy you. Know that it is an illusion, a belief that only makes it true if you believe it. The first six and a half years of grieving my daughter was in a dark corner at the back of my closet. My expectation of a lifetime of joys was destroyed when she died. I simply couldn't accept it, and there really was no one to hold me in this space, no one to validate my emotions, no one to walk with me on this path that I did not want to take.

I remember the moment that I met a woman who had a similar story to mine of her son's life and death. I knew in a blink of an eye that I was not alone, that there was someone who could see into the cracks of crevices of my heartache and know them like she knew her own. The feeling of comfort in this surrounded me and enveloped me in pure love, and a sigh left my lips in that moment, filled with all the feelings and echoes of my sorrow and despair. I am not alone. Her heartache is my heartache. Her grief is my grief. It didn't matter if she did or didn't believe in God, nor the differing details in our stories, I felt at one with her, knowing that she felt my sorrow, different or not. It is imperative to heal in a space where you are safe, where there is someone who truly feels your sorrow, who has been on the path of grieving a child, of a shattered life that lays on the floor after your child has died. Picking up the pieces is hard, with days that you can't bear to pick up a piece, and other days where you want to take the few large pieces and smash them to bits with rage. Then there are the days where you frantically try and piece the shards back together like a puzzle – the puzzle that was your life. Leave it where it lies. There is no going back. The life you thought you were creating wasn't meant to be. You have a new life, whether you want it or not. You can embrace it and wade through the murky waters, sinking to its depths. Or you can fight it with all you've got left in you, pushing it away, denying the truth for what it is and letting the rage take over your soul and dull every sense until it eats away at you. I chose to push it away for years, thinking that there was no other choice. It ate me alive, starving my soul, my body, my children's love – living every day in pain and despair, seeing through a bleak grey lens of isolation and a story that I didn't know how to change. It was not meant to be changed. It was meant to lead me to truth, to love, to life and, I see now, to lead me to you.

I don't want you to take the road I took. I want to tell you that you don't have to. I want you to know unequivocally that there is a space for you, for your sorrow and all the dreams and hopes that died with your child. I want you to know that there is hope, that you are loved and not alone. That there are shoulders to cry your tears on, and strength to be lent to you when you can't get up anymore. Know that death is not the end, that you are more loved and surrounded than ever before. Bad things do happen to good people and throughout history this has been recognized in some of the most horrific ways. Sometimes that bad thing's intention is to break you open, to show you how to flower, to be joy at the core of who you are, to shift your perspective of what life is really about or to bring you closer to your authentic self, that otherwise, would never have shown it's smile to face a day. The question is, which path will you choose? Will you open your heart to the pain in order to heal it, or shut it down with everything else in your life? The choice is yours and yours alone.

My wish for you is to show you that you actually have a choice, that you can choose for your heart to open. When you do, you are choosing to see through the lens of Spirit, the lens of your child's beautiful soul that is vibrating all around you – you are here, teetering on the edge of reality, the precipice of the meaning of death and life, the meaning of your purpose, your soul. You are here whether you want to be or not – the unknown gift in this tragedy is that the cage you've been unknowingly living in has just collapsed around you. No one tells you this fact, or acknowledges it for what it is. We are expected to try and fit back into the framework that has been caging us for our whole lives. Your cage has been broken open and know that you will feel naked, raw, like a speck of nothing in the universe that you thought was real. The sheer vulnerability in understanding this is so scary that you might wish the earth would swallow you whole, that you didn't have to face this. I promise you, if you face this, face the fear of the unknown, you'll wonder why you didn't choose it sooner. You've got nothing to lose – you've already lost the love of your life, the reason you got up every morning – you now have everything to gain. The choice is yours.

Walking through grief is a painful journey that is speckled with sheer joy and genuine laughter that bubbles unexpectedly out of the deepest hurts. It is an experience that forces you to examine everything your world is built on. Every expectation, every belief, every emotion and every moment of your life that brought you to this moment. Follow this. Question everything that is part of this experience. Ask the hard questions of yourself. The ones where your truth is laced with shame and guilt and there will be many that rear their face after a child dies. The weight of my answers was drowning me. Until I named them, acknowledged them, gave them a place in my soul to exist. The moment you can name it and feel it, is the moment you can love it and heal it. When you can love that pain, acknowledging everything that it is to you, the box it forced you to live in, then you can surrender to it and watch it melt away and the meaning come and go. You are here to learn to forgive yourself and understand that there are some things you do not have control over. There are some things in the moment that simply do not make sense, with the reason eluding you, evasive in every way. Learn to let go and trust the universe, your soul, and all that your life will bring you. But you have to let it come. Let the tears come when they start to burn your eyes. Don't apologize for being unable to form a sentence because the sobs are wracking your body so hard. Don't hide your words to make others more comfortable. It serves no one. Your truth, your story is a light that is waiting to be shone. It is what it is. If you honour it, you'll then be able to heal it.

Sometimes we get stuck in the feelings that we can't shine the light on. The feelings and thoughts that are dismissed or put in the closet because of the label that cages it. The cages that society has built don't allow you to step out of it or give you the choice to unlock it. We have become thousands of locked, carbon copy cages made of rules and expectations. What we don't realize is that each and every one of us has the key to the locks. Instead, we stay in our cages to make others happy, to keep the status quo, to ensure others are comfortable. It is stifling to the soul, to creativity, to desire, and to our perceived realities. It is no longer a secret that you have the key to your cage, that you have what you need to set yourself free. But very few know this. And even fewer, believe this. Sometimes, tragedy is the bringer of freedom from these cages we've built. It collapses under the weight of shocking truth and the paradigm of a perceived situation, and the stem from which the emotion grew and the reaction that is inevitable from the fractured beliefs we have.

Examining this concept allowed me to acknowledge that my cage was broken open by my daughter's death. But it was so painful and raw and with an unacceptable intensity for those around me, that I scrambled to try and rebuild the cage to what society expected it to be. All because I couldn't face the unknown, didn't recognize that I had a choice and no one could help me, understand me or know my sorrow. So I tried painstakingly to rebuild that cage with other people's blueprints, feelings, desires, and expectations. Only to have it blown open wide again by my daughter's father, seven years later. Thank God. I couldn't see the truth of my cage that I had locked myself into. I believed the lie that I was a victim and that I had no choice but to stay in those situations and feelings. But between the two of them, they broke it open for me. Each scored the pain, multiplying it, so that I had no choice but to feel it and to face it with the intensity of a hurricane. I wish I could say that I was a bigger person, an older soul, a more evolved human being, so that I could've recognized it the first time. But I wasn't. I was exactly what was expected of me, a photocopy, a product of society and its expectations and mass beliefs. Expectations are a cage in and of itself. But look deeper at this cunningly deceptive cage. We are taught to have expectations in everything. So how can an expectation hold you hostage like that? My daughter's whole life and future was based on expectations, from the second that we were aware she was conceived. Every mother does this, the joy of a newborn child unmatched and unforgettable, blissful in the thoughts of all that your lives will be together. Pure love. This is often what we expect our whole child's life to feel like to us. But the truth is that things are guaranteed to not go the way that you fantasize about, dream about. And their death is the dismantling of your cage. Gone are the familiar shackles as you are thrust into something that you never thought of, or could have even imagined was in your child's life plan, in your life plan. The cage of expectations is enormous, spreading the width of everything you know when your child dies. Let your cage of expectations lie broken beneath your feet. Looking back, I've come to the understanding that maybe the divine plan was for me to struggle in those cages, that there is no shame in my refusal to acknowledge the cage's existence. Maybe it is part of my story, my daughter's story, in order to bring it to light for others, if only to share it with you. To shed light on a difficult journey that is made harder by society's cages. So that you don't think you need to rebuild that cage. So that you know you have a choice.

The session that I attended at the request of my daughter and the kindness of Jade, was called a heal and release and was an immense help to me. A stepping stone, to healing my heart. It was diving into the thing, or the person, or the situation that was holding you hostage in your mind and in your emotions. For me it was the letting go of the anger and pain of losing my daughter, coupled with the anger at the detective for labelling me and that I allowed it to define me. It allowed me to give those feelings a voice and all that it meant. The rage, the unfairness, the loss, the life that would never be lived, and the people that hurt me instead of helping me. Putting the voice into words and writing them down, acknowledging them with burning tears as I wrote furiously. When I had spent every emotion, detailed every jagged shard of feelings, we lit those words on fire. Burned them with intention. Burned the emotions and these people that I could not let go of. As the paper burned, the words were burning and the emotions fell away from me, going up in flames with the paper. The emotions that I had bottled up, that I was drowning in, dissipated with the wind, floating away with each wisp of smoke. I surrendered to my truth of it all and gave it back to the universe, emotionally exhausted, with no judgement. Allowing what is, to be in existence so that it could float away. I left there feeling lighter, like I had healed some of the tears in my heart. I felt the blackness covering my heart gently sift away like sand in the wind. I slept like a baby that night. And that was the start of facing the pain, the grief, the love, the sorrow.

The reason I sought out the psychologist I mentioned before, was because of Ava's request for me to, because of her love letter to me. I'm grateful that I found a perfect fit for me, after experiencing poor counselling before this, filled with more blame and more damage, because they couldn't see the truth, couldn't let me be in the sorrow. An education and the designations and credibility it provides does not make someone a good counsellor, I've learned. Most times, we need a coach, a hand, specifically from someone who understands because they've been there. And then sometimes, like me, we are so broken and want to leave this life – that's when it is imperative to seek out a psychologist that can help you wade through the grief and all the things that surround it. Make sure that you seek out one that is a fit for you – meaning, one that holds the space for you, one that allows you to say all that is in your heart, no matter how shameful, how guilt ridden, or how wrong you think it is, and doesn't judge you. A trained and highly skilled psychologist can save your life *if* they are the right one for you. Dr. Harris helped me rebuild my life. She let me wallow in self-pity when I needed it and then spew forth all the rage that had been ignored for so long. She allowed me to be at my worst, at the bottom of the bottom, and she did this without judgement, without telling me how I should feel, without dismissing me. Dr. Harris held my hand when I needed it. Validated every feeling I felt in my grief. She allowed a safe space to voice my emotions and circumstances, something that no one had been able to provide me before. I feel a kinship with her as well, in the sense that she was able to pull from me the emotions when I was on the brink, and then soothe me when I just wasn't ready to face something. Dr. Harris used a methodology known as the concept of EMDR, also known as Eye Movement Desensitizing and Reprocessing, which is the process of reliving a particular event in your mind with all of the emotions and memories that come with it and then reprocessing it with different eye or hand movements, which over multiple sessions reduces the emotional distress of the memory or trauma, allowing you to move through it without it replaying the debilitating state that often accompanies trauma. A woman ahead of her time as she sought out and trained in this method of psychotherapy decades before. I cannot give enough praise or recommendation that you seek out a trained psychologist like this, if you need one. She gave me hope in people again, helped me rebuild trust in myself and set boundaries, to trust in the process of life despite the hurt and pain, to trust in God and the Universe again.

This allowed me to be me, which in turn guided me to realizations and those aha moments that traced back and delved into how I became this person sitting in her office, completely broken. I am grateful that she has been a part of my journey. I've learned much from her, and this was all thanks to my daughter, Ava. When I look back at my whole journey I can't help but notice and know deep in my heart that if someone had spent just a bit of time to hold that space for me, someone who had experienced the loss of their own child, someone who could shine a light in the darkness, someone who could honour my feelings and honour my child in that first year after she died … that my story likely wouldn't be the same, wouldn't have been so destructive or shaded by despair and sorrow that took over my life. It is glaringly obvious that there needs to be more bereavement coaches who provide a safe space, a place where it's okay to acknowledge and feel the true pain of losing a child.

When we acknowledge that all walls of our expectations, our lives, are down, then you can feel the unsteady step of true love and true sorrow. Let the ripple of fear help you to recognize that it is okay to go against the grain of expectation. It is okay to simply not be okay. It is okay to stumble on the new rocky landscape of your life. Everyone must stumble. It's how we learn to become adaptable, to go with the flow of the emotion. When I hear the stories of people who walk among us, that have stumbled, and learned and proved resiliency and profound love out of it, I can't help but be amazed for you and of you. Of all that you have been through. Even when the swell of emotion that takes you five steps back after you've worked so hard to take one half step forward. It can seem unending, unrelenting. It will get easier to walk through this when you let it exist, when you stop fighting it with every fibre of your being. When you see through your child's eyes you allow yourself to see the gift they have given to you, which is begotten out of pain. The deeper your sorrow, the greater your love is. And feeling both emotions, whenever they come up, will slowly bring you to a point of walking through both at the same time, delicately intertwined with the other and deeply fulfilling to your soul.

I am grateful for all that has transpired on my journey, despite the pain, the sorrow, the loss, my refusal to be a part of my story for years, and the denial of my truth. I sometimes sit in awe of the glistening web of life that weaves its path without reason or explanation until suddenly a strand breaks or is woven anew. And the bigger picture starts to make sense when you take a step back and observe, this is when you can see the past and how your life has mapped out so far. And you can also see that are many different paths that you can choose from as you move forward creating the rest of your map, the story of your life which is now in your hands. There are many paths that can help you on your journey. If you're reading this, maybe you haven't found a safe place, or a shoulder to cry on. Maybe the expectations and explanations you've been given by others just don't make sense, don't sit well in your bones. I have found a path that brings relief to the unrelenting sorrow of losing a child. A path that challenges our taught beliefs about death and removes the isolation and the taboo discussion that often follows the death of a child. I feel the pain of all that you have lost, what feels like the end of the story when it was supposed to be the beginning. Honour this in all its feelings. I'm right here with you. I invite you to seek out your truth and open yourself to the knowing that your child is alive and living in Spirit all around you – and to relish in the very feeling of that reality.

Chapter 11

Live, Laugh, and Love Again

"Out of suffering have emerged the strongest souls; the most massive characters are seared with scars."

– KHALIL GIBRAN

I've wondered to myself how the different healing points and discoveries on my path could be culminated together for other bereaved parents to help them heal. I wanted to share my journey with you so that you could learn what has brought me to joy and peace in the face of despair and sorrow, so that you too could live, laugh, and love again with more freedom and joy than you ever thought possible. If I can do this, you can do this. We all will grieve and yet we all have a different journey through grief, different meanings and darkened tunnels that we must take. For some the path is brightly lit and a hand guides them around the stones of despair wedged into the path they are walking. And yet for others, it is fraught with giant sink holes in the earth that they will fall into because they cannot see the light, do not have a guiding hand to help them. What is the difference between the two people? I think it is partly who they are, what their life experience has been – was it filled with love or filled with torment and negativity? Are they open to themselves, to the truth, or is there a hidden agenda deep in their subconscious, an excerpt from the tape of society's dysfunction? And most importantly, do they feel safe enough to examine every belief they have? The simple answer is that it is a choice. You are the person who decides how your story will unfold. You can choose to uncover your truth or leave it buried with despair and sorrow. Every moment in your life is an opportunity to change your understanding, to shift your perspective – to be the hero of your own story, to decide if you want to be happy. So, which one will you choose, the victim or the hero? Despair or joy? Ask yourself this – which one would my child want me to choose? They'd choose hero and joy for you every time.

It was no coincidence that my son wanted me to get a boat license out of the blue - buying my sailboat was the push I needed to choose to be my own hero, the writer of the rest of my story, a story that I choose, filled with love and joy. How interesting that grieving and sailing have so much in common, a similar wisdom and alchemy within them both, running parallel to each other. The storm is often used in our attempts to describe the deepest hurts in our souls, the ebb and flow of the journey of life. No matter what the storm, no matter what point in your life, there is a gift held within every storm, swirling around waiting for you to see it, to be washed ashore, broken open, but with a treasure, the gift of that storm. In the midst of a life storm we are often called to trust the divine and the unknown why of circumstance, yet few of us do. Instead we are plagued with worry and devising plans to attempt to control the damage, change the possible outcomes. But, if you simply trusted, took the hand of Spirit, and let it guide you blindly, you would come out the other side much easier and with gifts aplenty. When we can do this, the life storm will blow us around but it will not destroy us, because we are allowing ourselves to be held in the infinite. Instead you are given refuge in God, in Spirit because you are trusting the divine regardless of the situation or circumstance that surrounds you. Just like the boat we sit upon amidst the vast waters of the ocean. When a storm rolls up to you on the ocean, naturally you would hunker down in the cabin and close the doors. The boat would rock fiercely tossing you about the cabin. And you have two choices. The one most of us make, is to keep your eyes wide open, filled with fear and trying to contain the tossing, scrambling to stand firm when there is no way to stand firm in that place, in that moment, making yourself sick in the process. The second choice is much like following the divine, having faith and closing your eyes, trusting that although you will be tattered, you will still be afloat and not worrying and making yourself sea sick in the process. I choose to grieve and live in the divinely trusted boat, not the one that I am trying to control and filled with fear.

There are many gifts the death of a child can bring you. Yes, this is a hard concept to wrap your brain around when you've lost a child. And yes, I fought it too, and said, clearly that person has never held their child as they took their last breath, they don't understand. I failed miserably, not seeing any life, any gift, because I couldn't move past the pain, couldn't face it. The failure of fighting the truth of that statement almost killed me. I want you to see that there is no end of life and no prize for sitting in the despair and unfairness of your loss for so long that it eats away at your soul. I promise you, the gifts are there. They are waiting for you to pick up the rubble, uncovering your truth. Begging you to dust off the soot and shine the light on your truth, on your child's life.

I wrote this book to tell the truth about life after losing a child. The truth of grieving in such a displaced and fragmented way. I wanted to shine a light on how our cultural beliefs result in so many of us not being able to grieve due to the lack of support and our dysfunctional beliefs. The result of this is felt at the core of who we are, the abandonment, the inability to move forward, to forgive, to love again. At times, we are shunned as bereaved parents because we are so broken, hidden away in our sorrow – but that is not how we can heal and it does nothing but make the pain greater for us. I want to talk about the uncomfortableness our society has about death so that all can see my daughter's truth, my truth. So that the fear of death doesn't cage us into misery and despair anymore. I wanted to point out all of the things we have been taught that only give more dysfunction, more fear and end up disabling people's ability to accept and grieve a child. My child is dead and this is what life can be like when you live in a culture that regulates the meaning of death and pushes your soul back into a cage. It doesn't feel safe to be a broken parent, to have lost what no one wants to lose. It is all wrong. We are taught a backwards education that judges us, then numbs us and then medicates us, only to dismiss us when those things don't work. Don't let this define you. See it when it happens and acknowledge it for what it is, a road block to show you a deeper level of beliefs that you need to look at. The truth of knowing this allows you to walk around that trap.

All of the exercises and tips in this book can be done individually to help you. You can do them while you read each chapter, or in your own time when you are ready. Sometimes the best time is when your struggle requires you to face yourself. I want your struggle with this loss to be soothed in its darkest moments, your heart to be filled with hope again, and your soul comforted with the truth of unending life.

Let your heart swell with greater joy than it ever has before and cry tears of happiness at feeling the connection with your child. That is my vision – to heal shattered hearts from this loss and mend it back together with hope and truth and love. To connect you with your child, to show you a truth in this world of life and death. I have experienced this and been able to move forward, without the weight of tragedy, without the blanket of despair, with deeper love and purpose and knowing. I want you to experience this too, for yourself. So that you can feel the joy in the sorrow and be held in the infinite hands of the universe, feeling safe and loved and more whole than you'd ever believe.

I believe that we can face this and make it better for all those who will walk this path of losing a child. I believe that if we shine the light on the things that separate us from love, from wholeness, from tears, from grief, then we can all come together so that no one is alone, no one is isolated, and no one is kicking them when they are down. I have experienced the grace and joy in being able to heal with a new understanding of society and death. I'm so fortunate that this is my story and my daughter blessed my life. The gratitude I have, now settled deeply in my bones, knowing that I have come through my darkest hours and deepest sorrows, a better person, with purpose and passion and a love of life that I have never had before. Yes it came from circumstances and pain that no parent would wish for and that I would not wish on any soul. But the truth is I've been given the greatest gifts, it was just a question of seeing them, of seeing the truth. I could never have learned these lessons or earned these gifts without the experience of my story. From pain was born love and joy. It has given me unparalleled pleasure and a deeper love for the universe and our connections to each other. I wish the same for you. I hope you'll open your heart to all that the universe and Spirit has waiting for you. I hope that you'll join me on a healing retreat to be soothed by connecting with others who share your grief, and that you will feel the splendour and elation that follows meeting your child again. This is a space that I created to listen with my whole heart to your sorrow and the heartache of your unique circumstances and your child's beautiful soul. To teach you the methods that I learned through my journey that were powerfully transforming and healing. To help you discover that nothing is what it seems and that there is great joy waiting for you, if you're willing to do the work, explore your heart and all you believe. To give you permission to voice your pain and let your grief be heard from the depths of your soul. To offer you a space for your broken heart that is safe and surrounded by those who have walked this journey and have come through the other side more whole than you'd ever imagined. You have been given a gift, but it is up to you to uncover it – know that you are worthy of these gifts.

You are worth it. When you've lost the dearest part of yourself, you have an opportunity to live life, laugh, and love again. Sometimes you just need a little help finding the gifts in your sorrow. You've got nothing left to lose. Your life can be magical if you allow it, and you can decide to start your healing process anytime, any place. I hope my story has helped you in some way. Whether it brought comfort to you, or validated your experience in some way. I hope that it has opened your heart to the new life that awaits you. I know that you have the courage and strength in you to take that first step to healing your broken heart whether on your own journey or joining me on a healing retreat that is designed to help heal your heart, uncover your authentic self, and connect you with your child. You've already experienced the worst of loss, why not experience the love and the gift of this, that is still waiting for you.

Live, Laugh, and Love again.

Love Ava and Erin

Acknowledgments

I am truly blessed with a support network that so few people have in this life. My family and close friends have been my witnesses, my supporters, the soothers of my tears, the net that has caught me after I've fallen. I am forever grateful to be sharing this journey of mine and theirs together. I could never have come this far on my journey without all of them. They all have played an integral role in my life and helped the puzzle pieces come together. Your hearts dwell in my heart, always and forever.

Mom and Dad, I clearly wouldn't be where I am today without the two of you. Thank you for walking beside me when all was lost. For cheering me on and helping me look forward when I could only look back. Thank you for loving all of me, the light and the dark, and the oh so vast grey areas in between.

Jennifer, my sister, my best friend, my defender and my total opposite. You are the yin to my yang in so many ways. You are always being my big sister, even though you are my little sister. Thank you for being the kindest and gentlest soul with me. Thank you for your unending positiveness you give me. For loving my children like they are your own. For being exactly who you are. You have no idea how amazing you are.

Maureen, you are an up-lifter of souls, a grand life observer like the wisdom of the hawk and a philosopher of the many lives you've lived. You are my tribe. I'm honored that you chose me to share your journey with. I'm elated and grateful to have a true friend who empowers me to be authentic, to rise up and to see all of the things you see in me. I can only hope to do the same for you in this lifetime.

Evan, we've shared the worst of the worst that can happen in life. The perils and heartbreak that plagued our life and relationship together have taught me so much. I would never have learned without you playing your own part in the chaos, it gave me the ultimate gift of myself again. Thank you for showing me my worth. Thank you for creating doors for me that I never even knew existed. I wish you great peace, bright shining lights to show you the way and for true unconditional love to surround you for the rest of your life. You will always hold a place in my heart.

Dr. Harris, you were the heart that held my broken heart without judgement or disconnect. Thank you for helping me weed the garden of my soul and unearthing the gifts that helped me to plant an abundance of new loving seeds.

Tiffany, you are my knight in shining armor. A timed connection only the divine could've orchestrated. Thank you for listening to your soul, to Spirit, and the universe. Thank you for your courage to step up and for being the vessel to help heal my heart with your gifts. You are one of a kind, so keep shining your light for it is a beacon of hope for the broken-hearted and bereaved. You are giving a gift that is priceless.

To the Morgan James Publishing team: Special thanks to David Hancock, CEO & Founder for believing in me and my message. To my Author Relations Manager, Tiffany Gibson, thanks for making the process seamless and easy. Many more thanks to everyone else, but especially Jim Howard, Bethany Marshall, and Nickcole Watkins.

Dr. Angela Lauria and her team, thank you for helping me find my voice, face my fears and summon the courage to 'show up'. This book wouldn't be possible without all of you. Thank you for giving me the permission and encouragement I needed to say 'this is me' – Thank you from the bottom of my heart.

About the Author

Erin is a bereaved mother and spent years suffering alone in her grief. Like many parents, she found the struggles of life after losing a child, the physical, emotional, and mental effects of anger and grief unexpressed, debilitating.

Trained as a peer group facilitator for grieving individuals, Erin is passionate about providing other grieving parents a different path to heal in a more healthy and spiritual way through retreats for bereaved parents that empower them to know they can be fulfilled, feel love deeply again, and find true peace in the midst of one of life's greatest losses.

Erin is living life with peace and joy, residing in the region of Waterloo, Canada. She lives with her two beautiful children and beloved family dog, Daisy and loves spending time on their family's sailboat on Lake Erie.

Thank You!

I sincerely hope that Ava's story and mine have helped you in some way on your journey through grief. I know that living in grief without the right support or help is a life full of suffering, a life of pain and sorrow.

Now you know that there is another way to get through this.

As a thank you for reading Love You, Ava Baby, my personal gift to you is a free session about ending hopelessness after child loss. This session is the first step in easing your pain and finding your way, no matter where you are in your journey through grief, no matter how broken and hopeless you feel.

Connect with me to schedule your free session today.

Website: www.ThereisLifeafterLosingaChild.com

Facebook: LoveyouAvaBaby

Email: info@loveyouavababy.com